EASY PIANO

JOSH GROBAN NOËL

ISBN 978-1-4234-5685-8

HAL•LEONARD® CORPORATION

7777 W. BLUEMOUND RD. P.O. BOX 13819 MILWAUKEE, WI 53213

Visit Hal Leonard Online at
www.halleonard.com

NOËL

CONTENTS

SILENT NIGHT

Traditional
Arranged by DAVID FOSTER
and JORDAN D. FOSTER

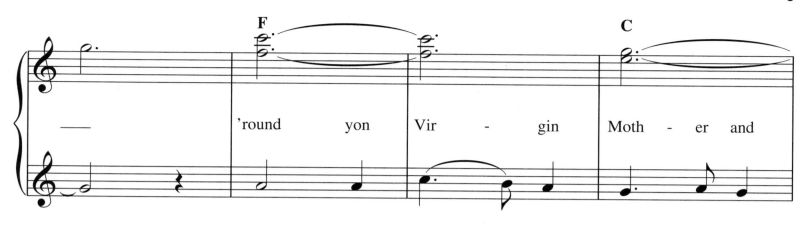

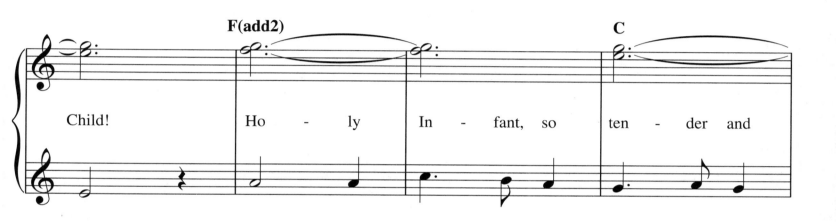

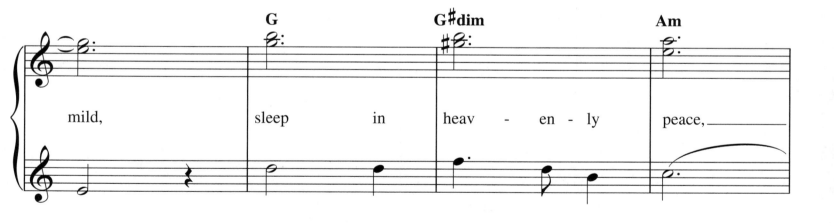

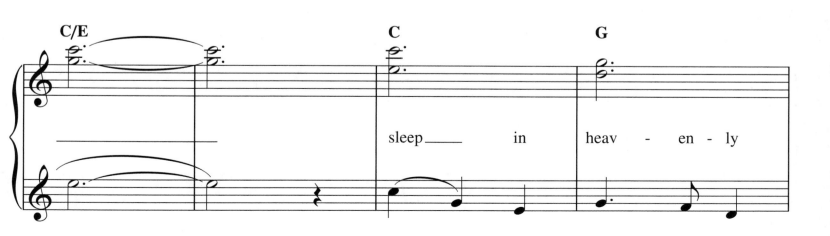

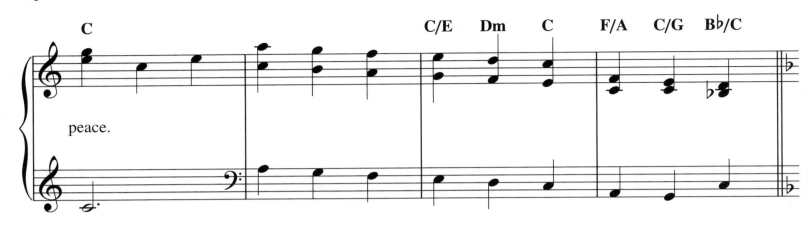

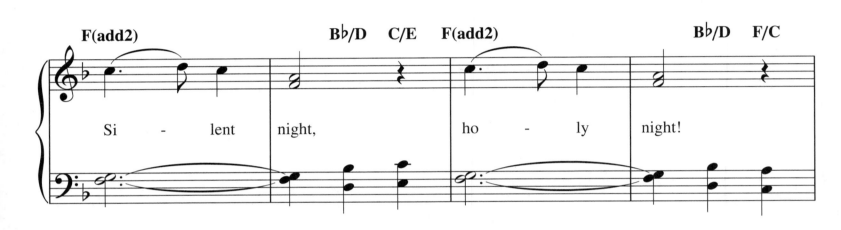

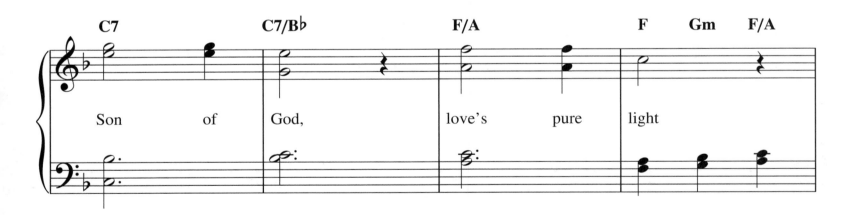

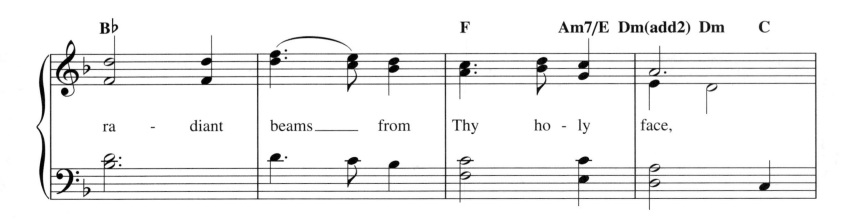

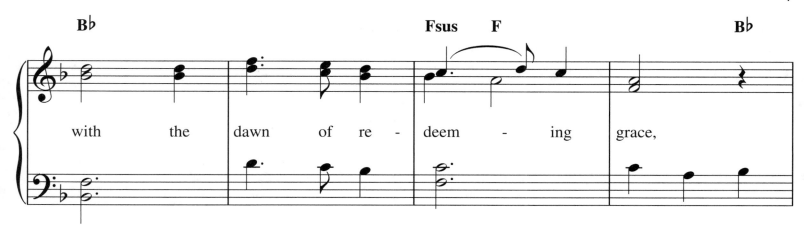

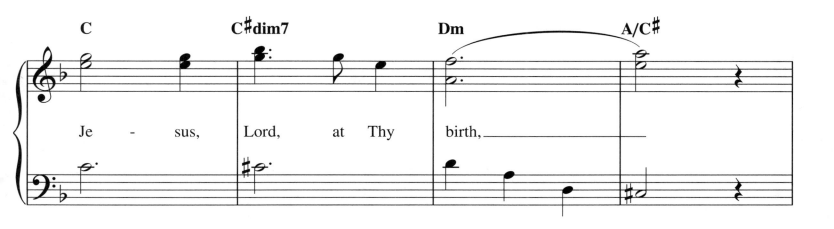

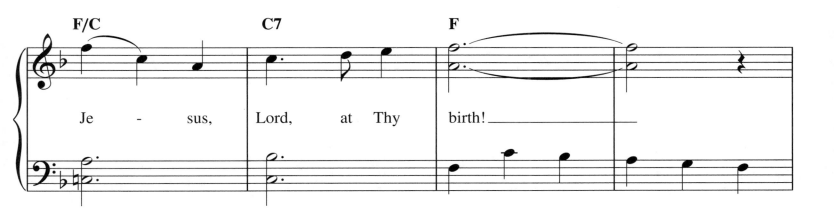

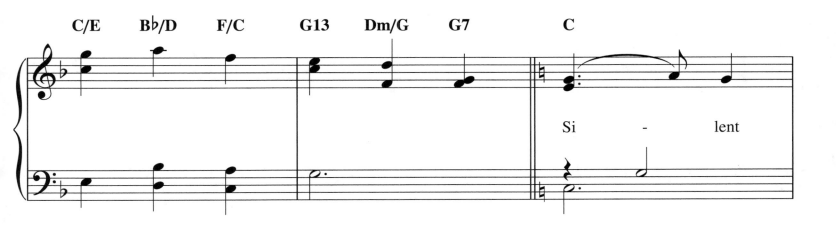

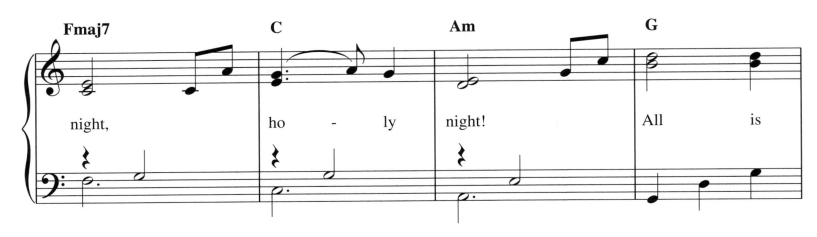

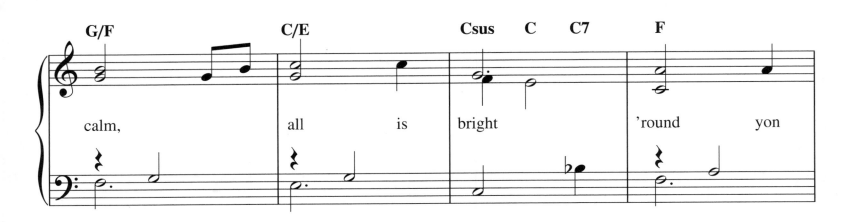

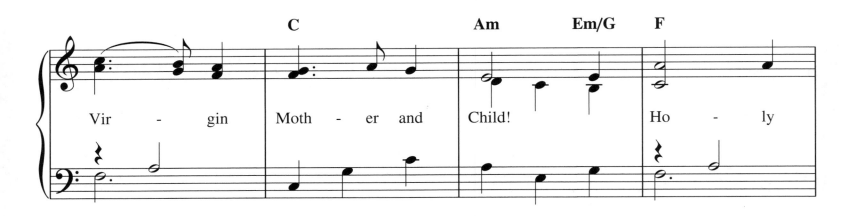

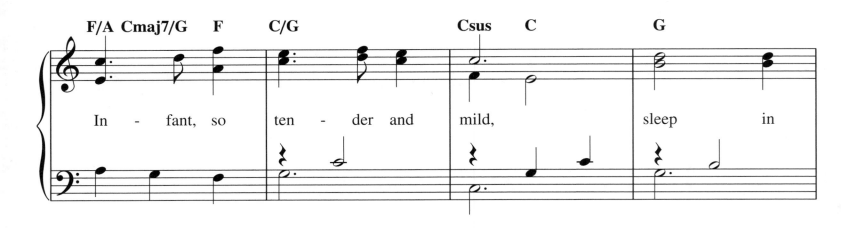

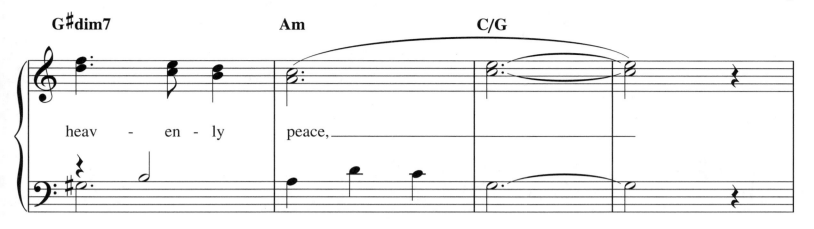

G#dim7 **Am** **C/G**

heav - en - ly peace,_____

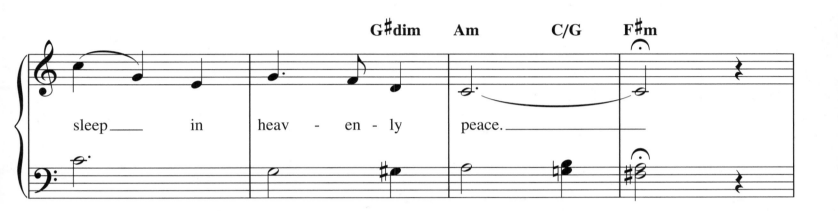

G#dim **Am** **C/G** **F#m**

sleep_____ in heav - en - ly peace._____

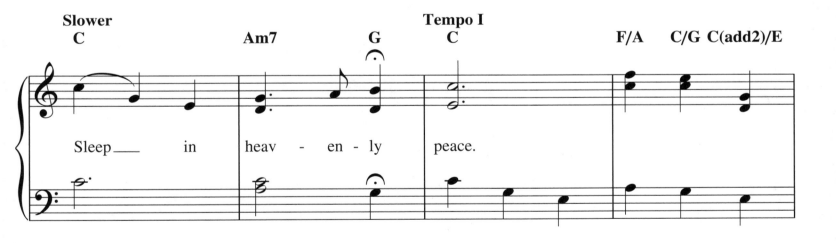

Slower
C **Am7** **G** **Tempo I** **C** **F/A** **C/G** **C(add2)/E**

Sleep_____ in heav - en - ly peace.

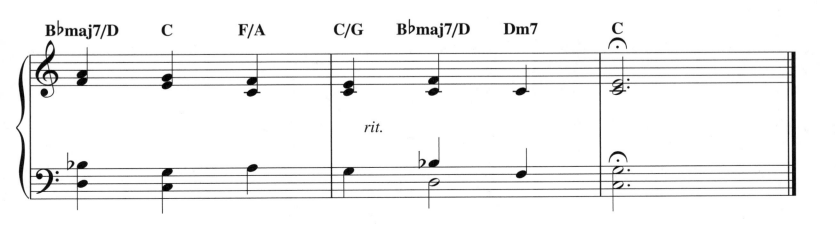

B♭maj7/D **C** **F/A** **C/G** **B♭maj7/D** **Dm7** **C**

rit.

THE LITTLE DRUMMER BOY

Words and Music by KATHERINE K. DAVIS,
HENRY ONORATI and HARRY SIMEONE

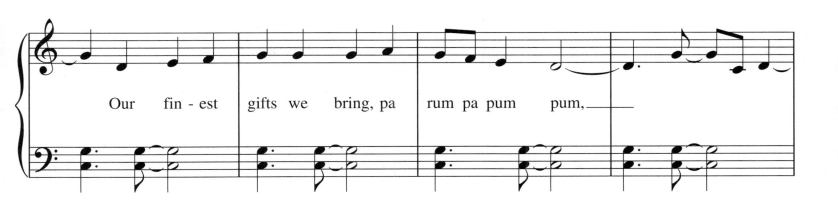

Lit - tle

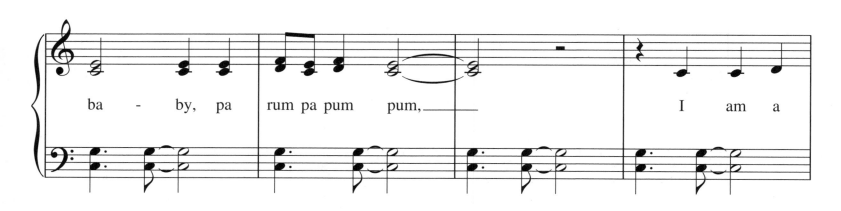

ba - by, pa rum pa pum pum, ___ I am a

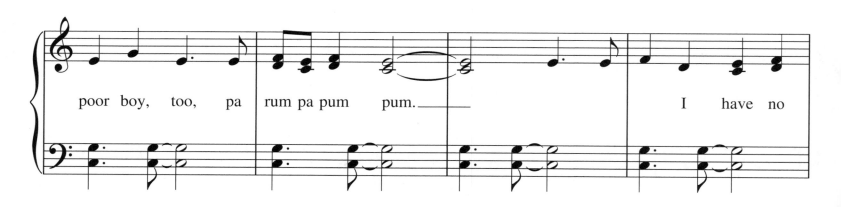

poor boy, too, pa rum pa pum pum. ___ I have no

G

gift to bring, pa rum pa pum pum, ___ that's fit to

give a King, pa | rum pa pum pum, | rum pa pum pum, | rum pa pum pum.

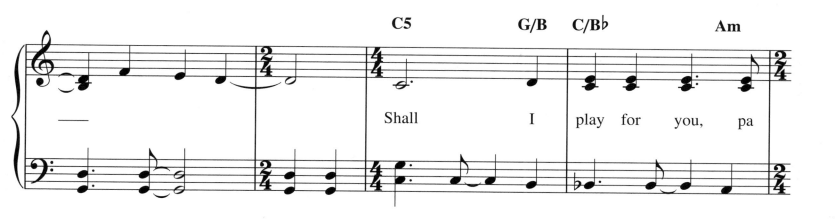

Shall | I play for you, pa

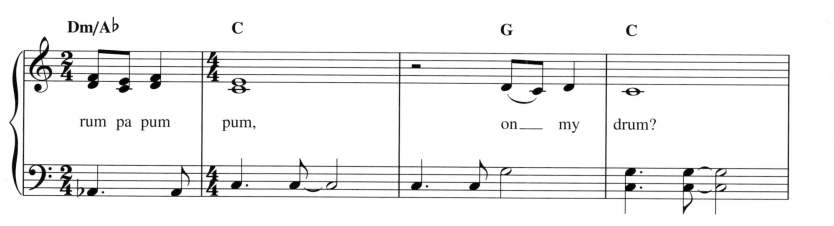

rum pa pum | pum, | on__ my | drum?

On__ my__ drum._____

I play my drum for Him.____

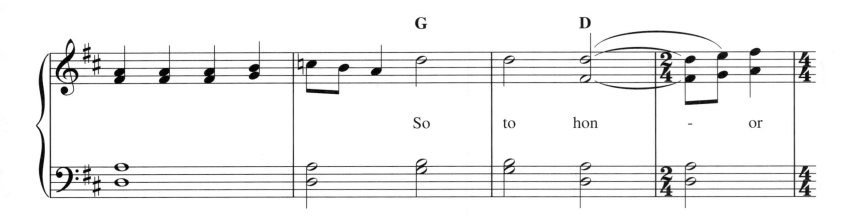

So to hon - or

15

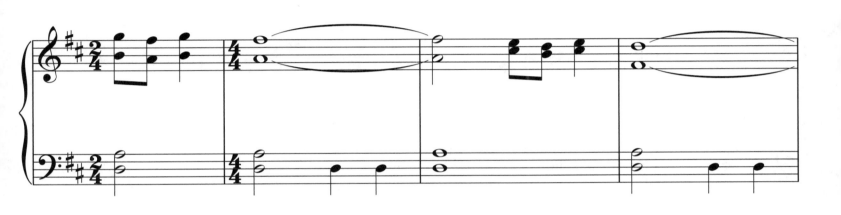

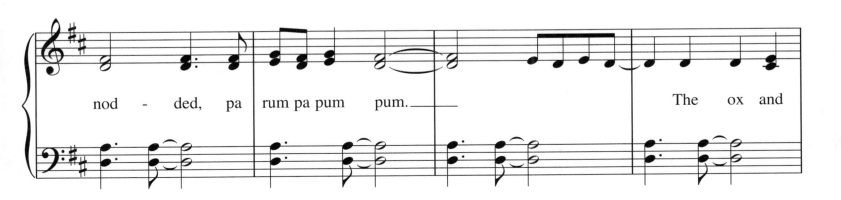

16

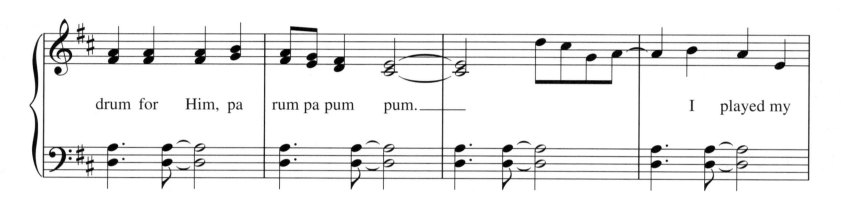

I'LL BE HOME FOR CHRISTMAS

Words and Music by KIM GANNON
and WALTER KENT

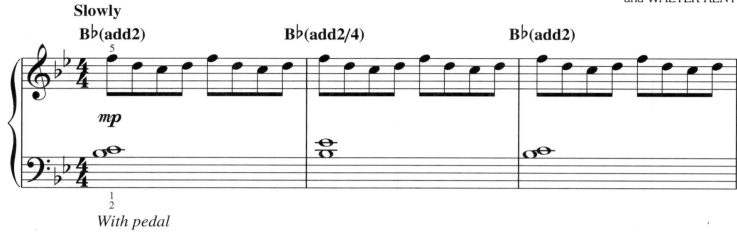

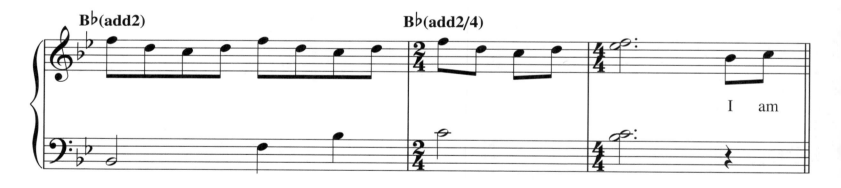

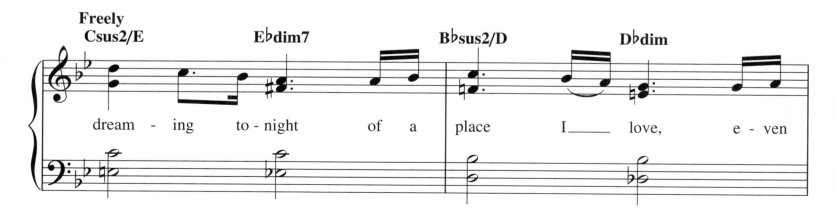

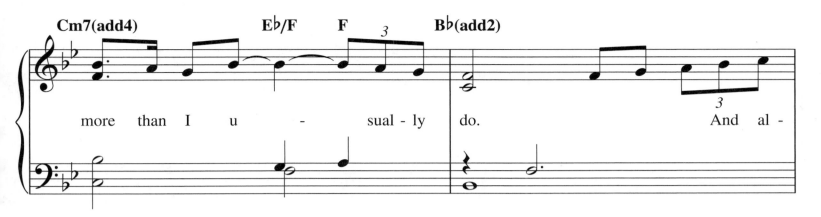

Cm7(add4)   **E♭/F**   **F**   3   **B♭(add2)**

more than I u - sual - ly do.   And al -

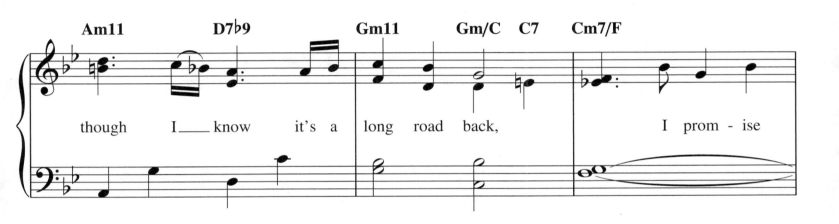

Am11   **D7♭9**   **Gm11**   **Gm/C**   **C7**   **Cm7/F**

though I___ know it's a long road back,   I prom - ise

F   **Slowly**   **B♭(add2)**   **Dm7**   **D♭dim7**

you: I'll be home for

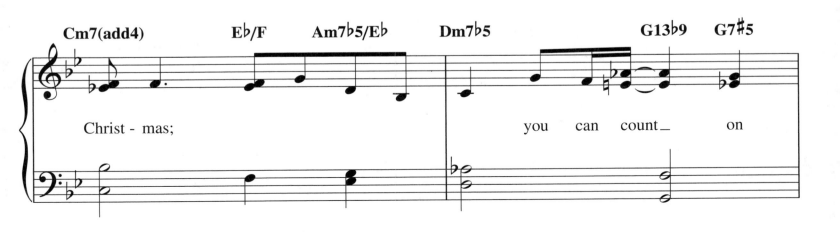

Cm7(add4)   **E♭/F**   **Am7♭5/E♭**   **Dm7♭5**   **G13♭9**   **G7♯5**

Christ - mas;   you can count___ on

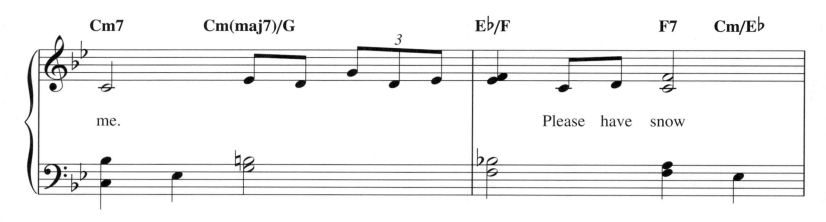

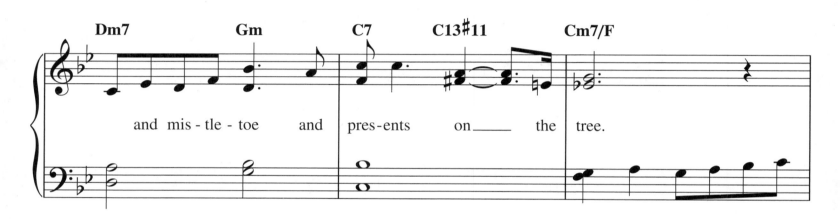

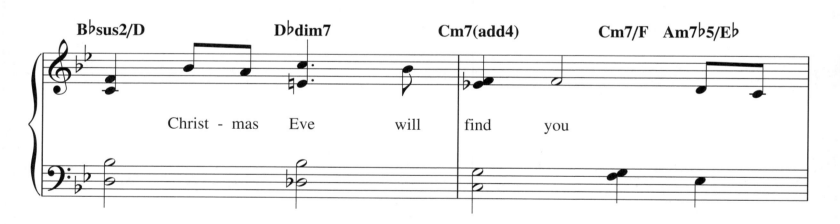

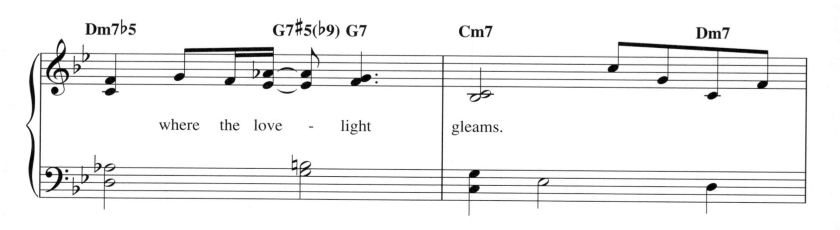

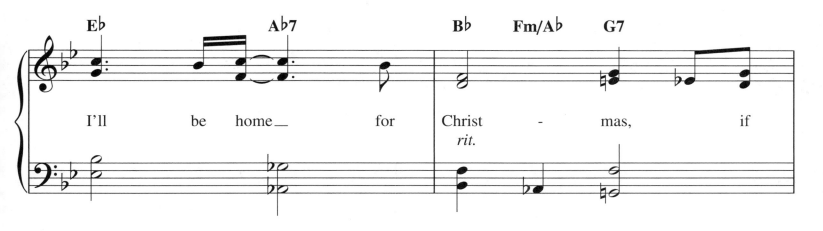

I'll be home for Christ - mas, if

on - ly in my dreams.

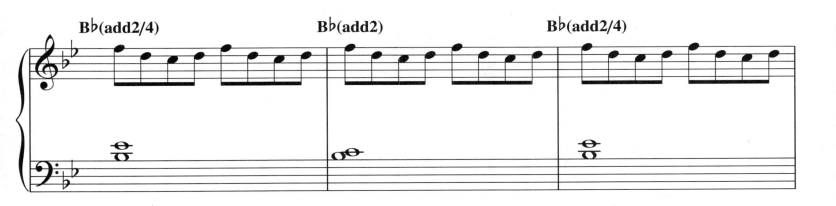

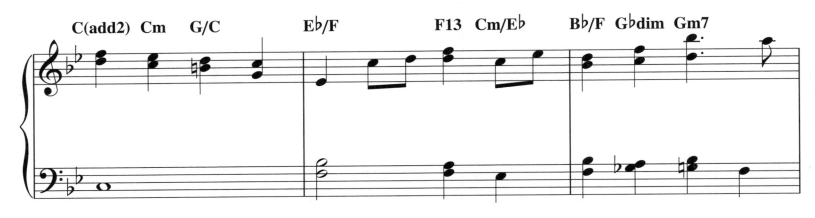

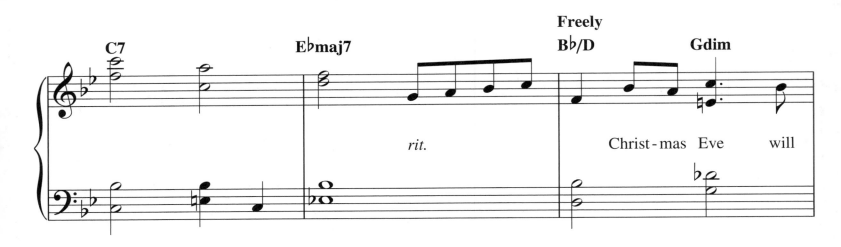

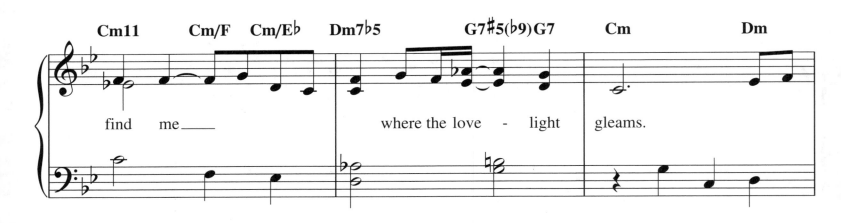

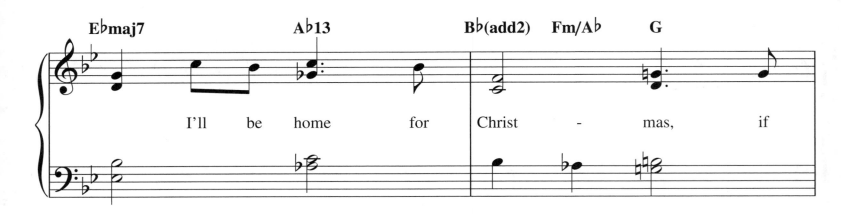

only in my dreams, if

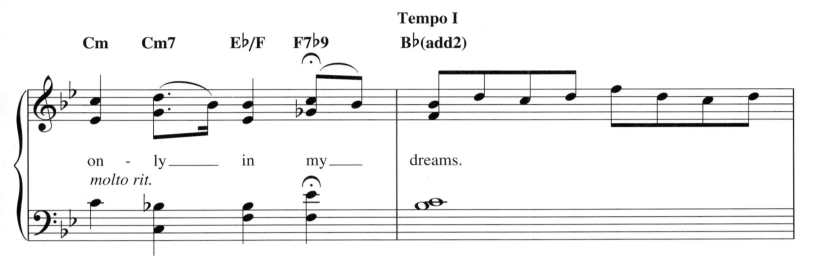

Tempo I

only in my dreams.

molto rit.

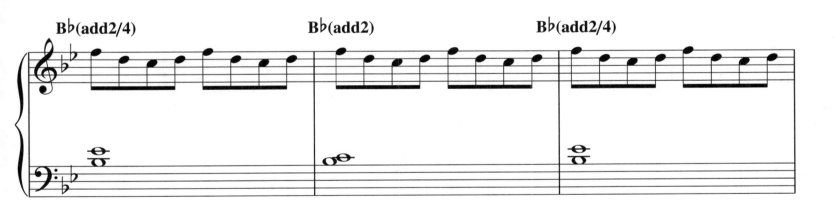

rit.

AVE MARIA

Traditional
Arranged by DAVID FOSTER
and JORDAN D. FOSTER

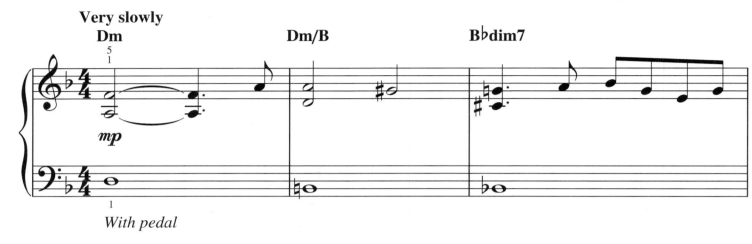

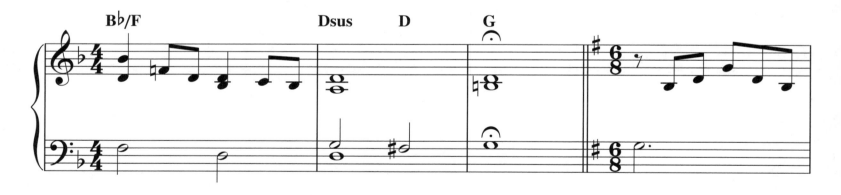

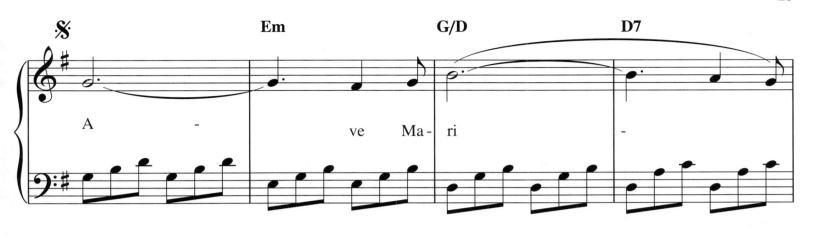

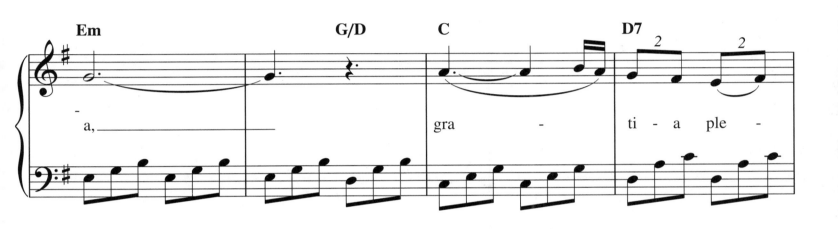

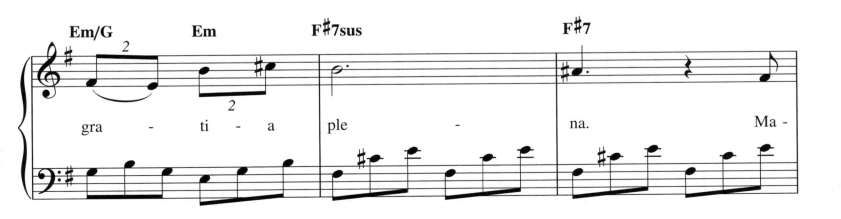

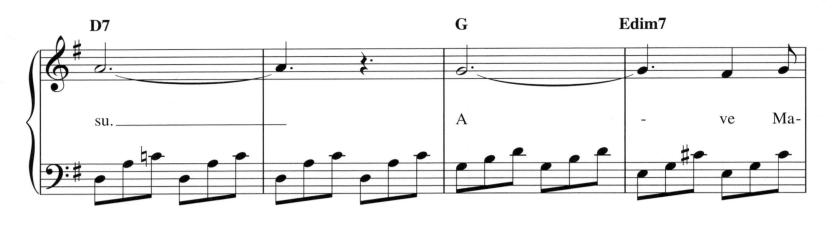

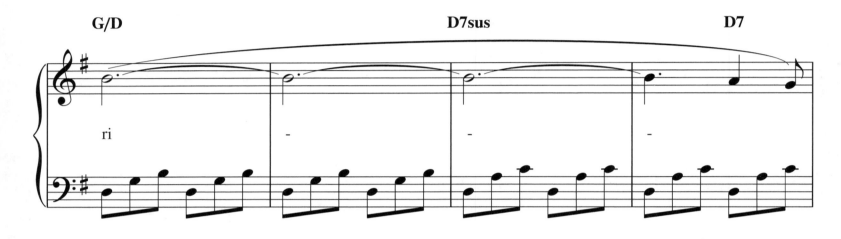

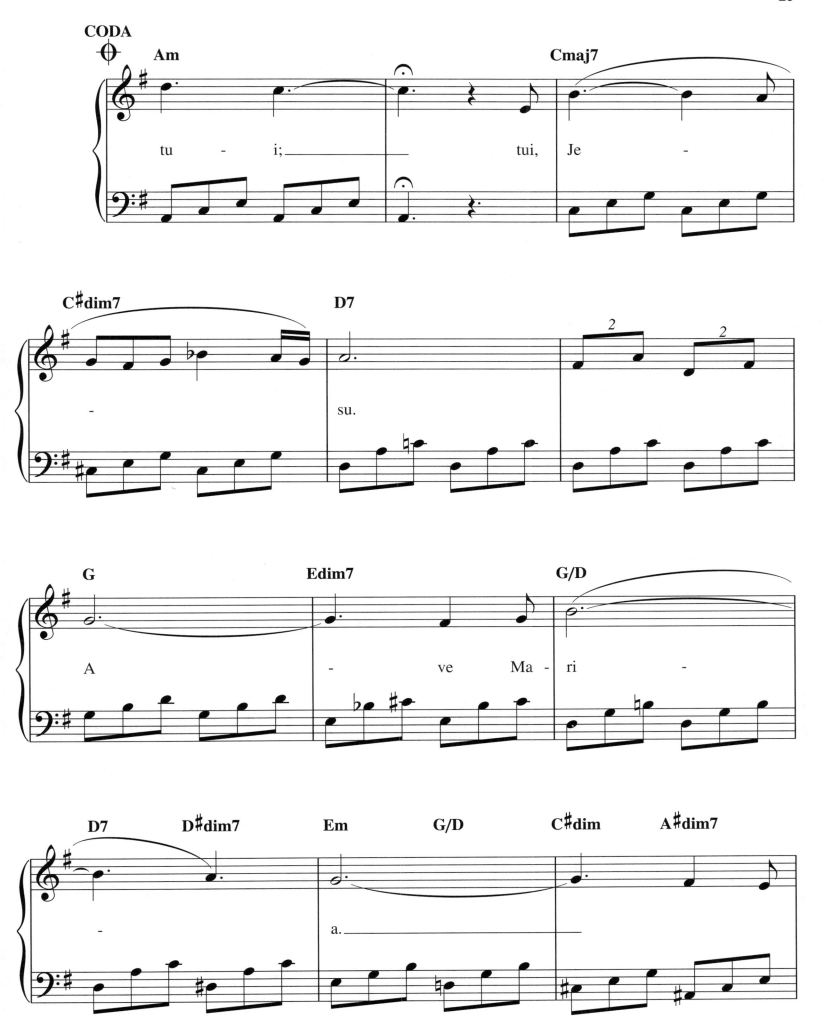

THANKFUL

Words and Music by CAROLE BAYER SAGER,
DAVID FOSTER and RICHARD PAGE

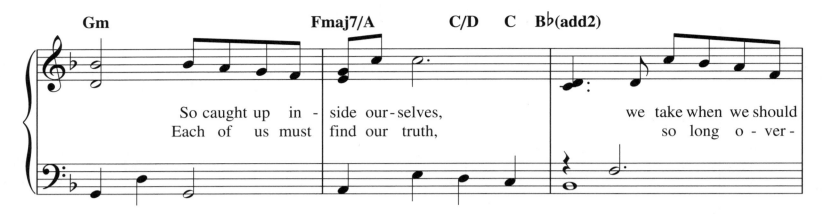

So caught up in - side our - selves,
Each of us must find our truth,
we take when we should
so long o - ver -

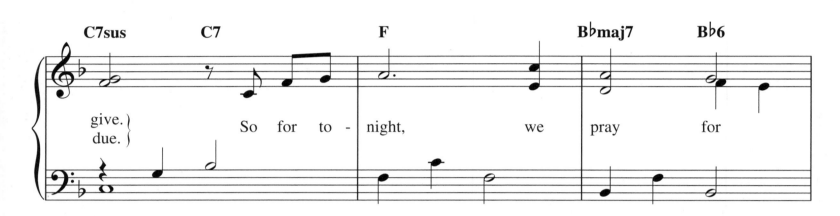

give.
due.
So for to - night, we pray for

what we know can be.
{And on this}
{And ev - 'ry} day we

hope for what we still can't see. It's up to

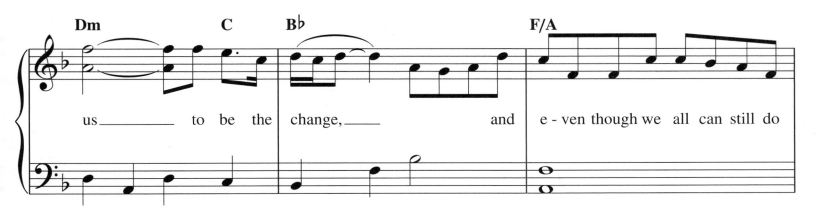

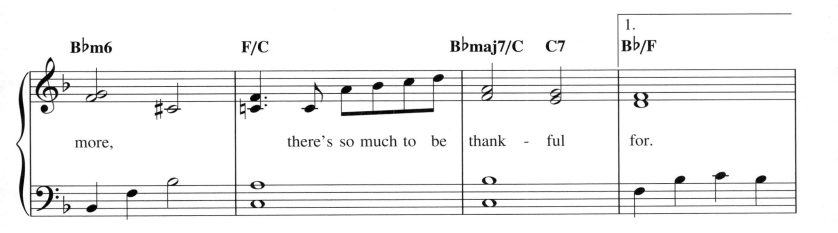

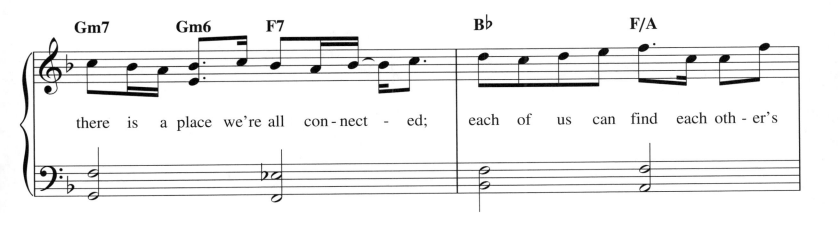

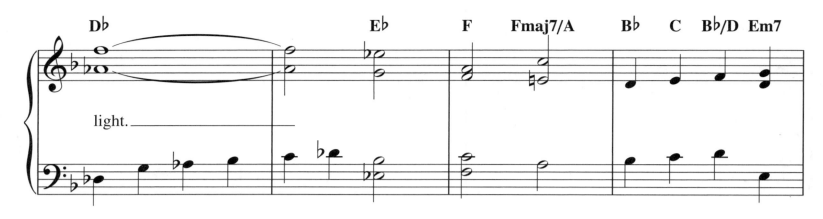

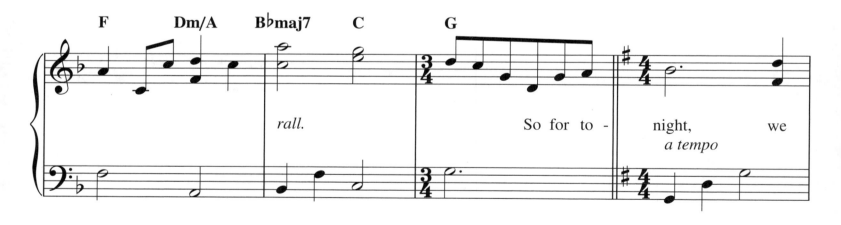

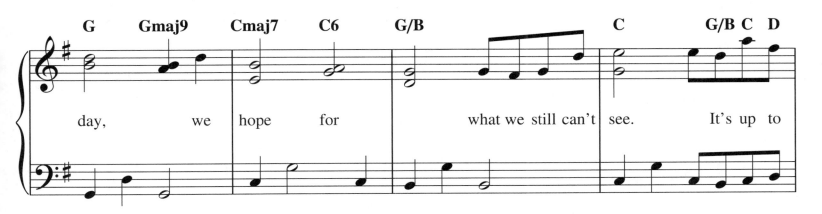

day, we hope for what we still can't see. It's up to

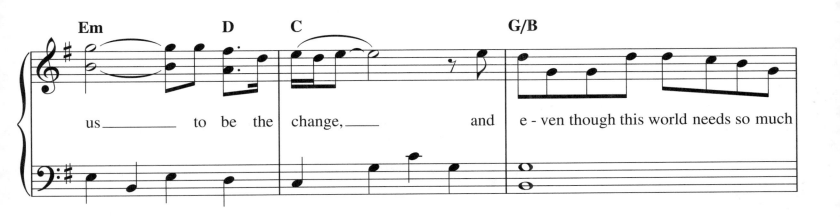

us____ to be the change,____ and e - ven though this world needs so much

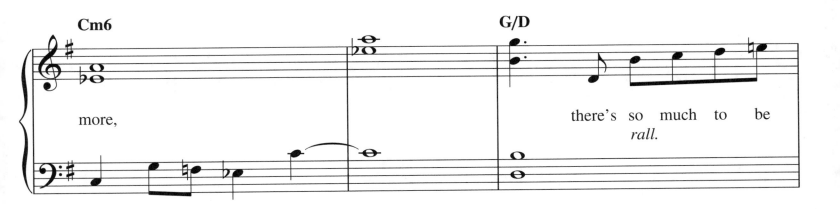

more, there's so much to be

rall.

thank - ful for.

a tempo

ANGELS WE HAVE HEARD ON HIGH

Traditional
Arranged by DAVID FOSTER
and SARAH MICHAEL FOSTER

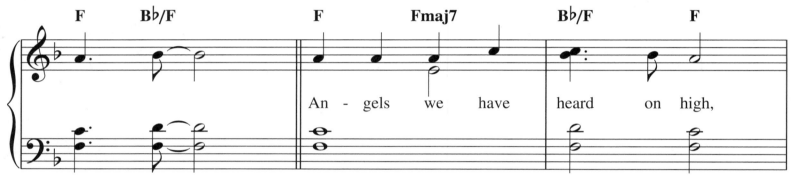

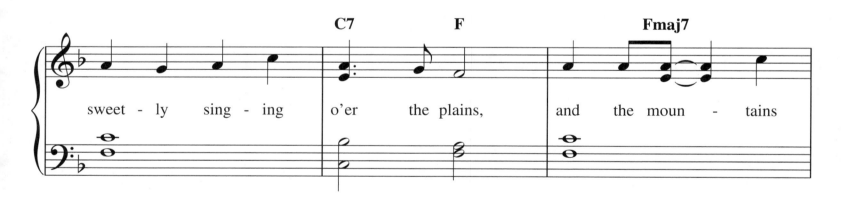

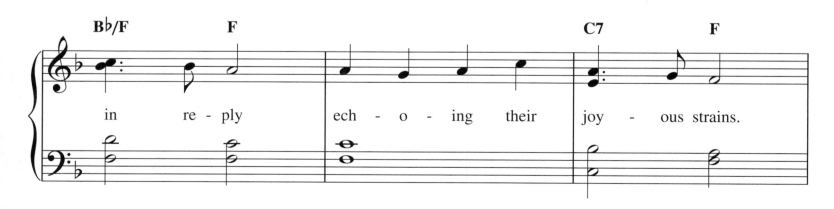

Come to Beth - le - hem___ and see___

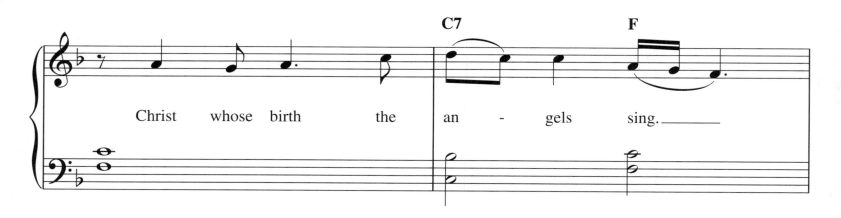

Christ whose birth the an - gels sing._____

Come a - dore_____ on___ bend - ed knee___

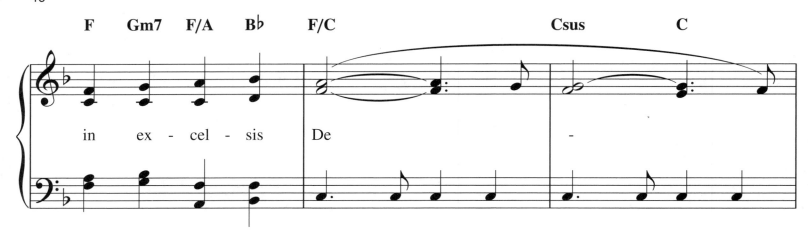

in ex - cel - sis De

o.

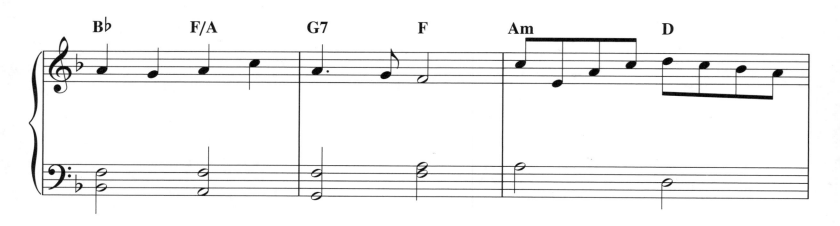

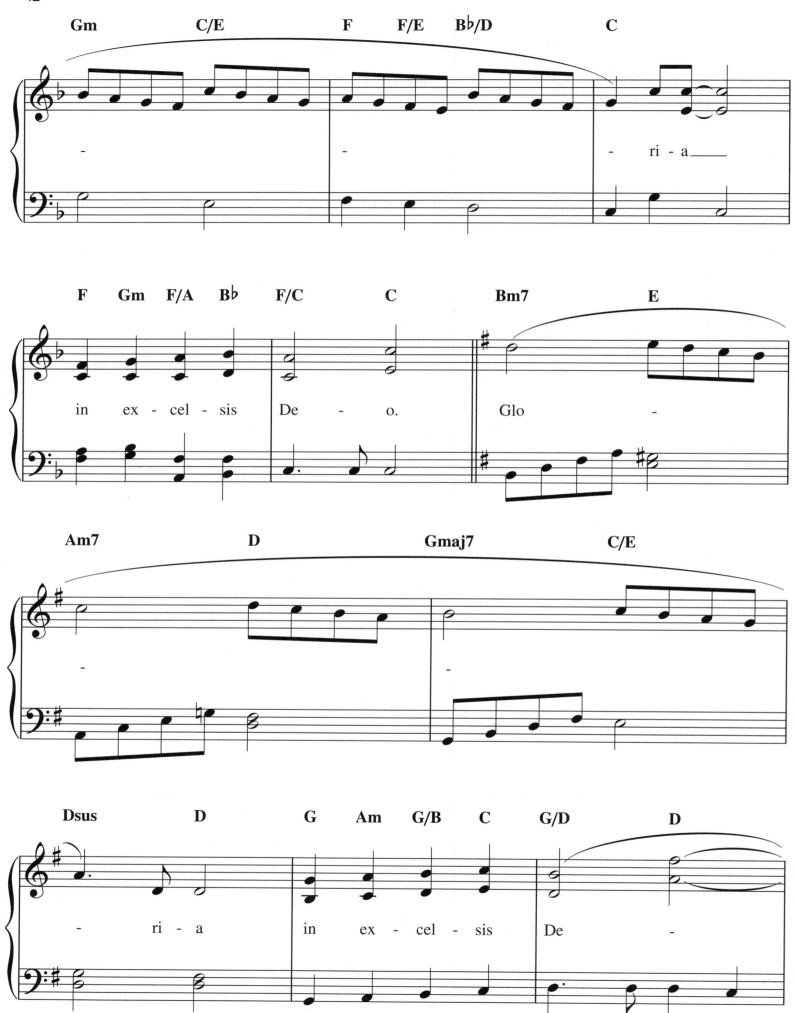

THE CHRISTMAS SONG
(Chestnuts Roasting on an Open Fire)

Music and Lyric by MEL TORMÉ
and ROBERT WELLS

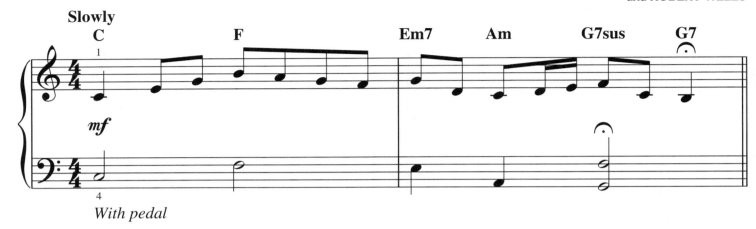

Chest - nuts roast - ing___ on an o - pen fire,

Jack Frost nip - ping___ at your nose, yule - tide car - ols be - ing

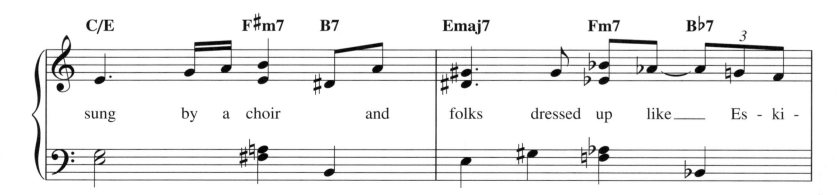

sung by a choir and folks dressed up like___ Es - ki -

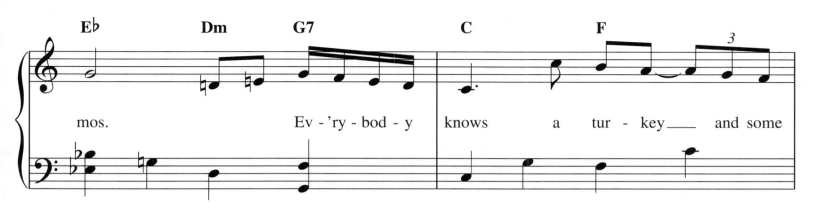

mos.   Ev -'ry - bod - y knows a tur - key___ and some

mis - tle - toe   help to make___ the sea - son bright.

Ti - ny tots___ with their eyes all a - glow___ will find it hard___ to sleep to -

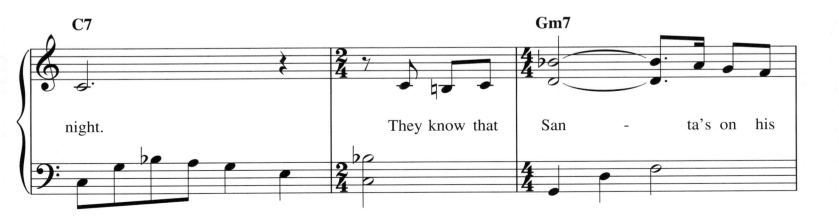

night.   They know that San -   ta's on his

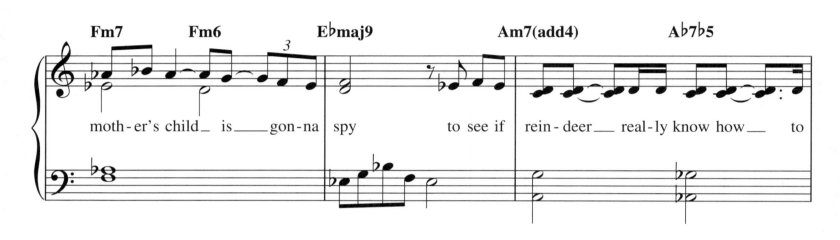

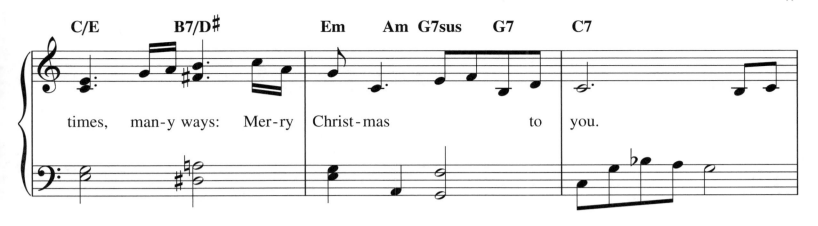

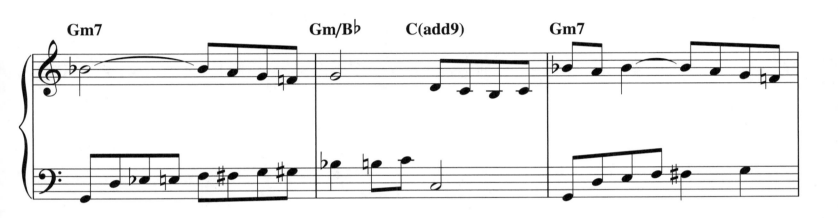

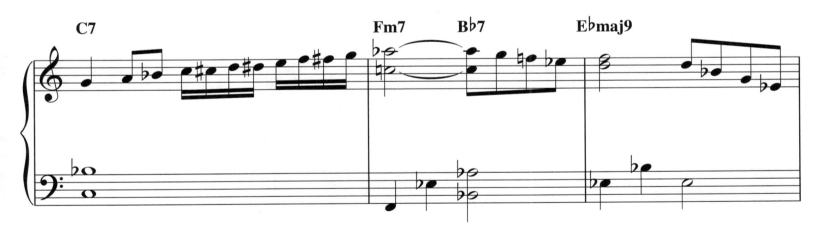

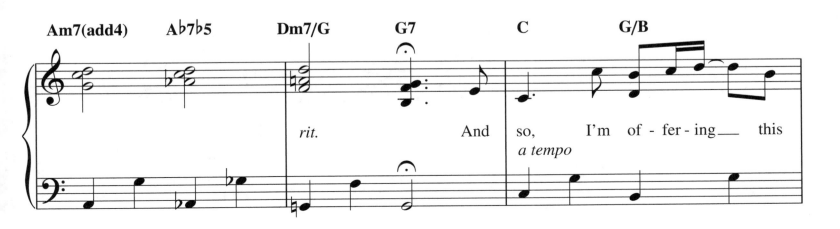

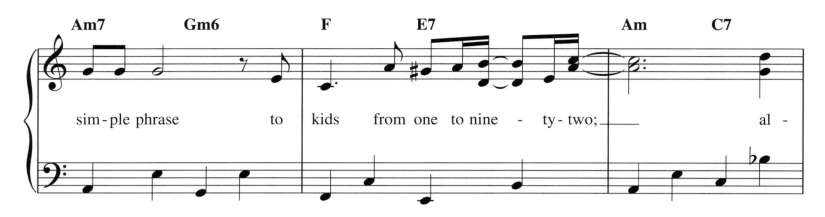

sim-ple phrase   to   kids   from one to nine - ty-two; _____   al -

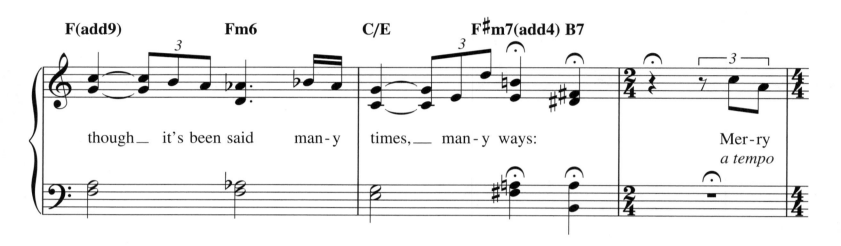

though__ it's been said   man - y   times,__ man - y ways: Mer - ry
a tempo

Christ - mas, ____   Mer - ry Christ - mas   to __
rit.

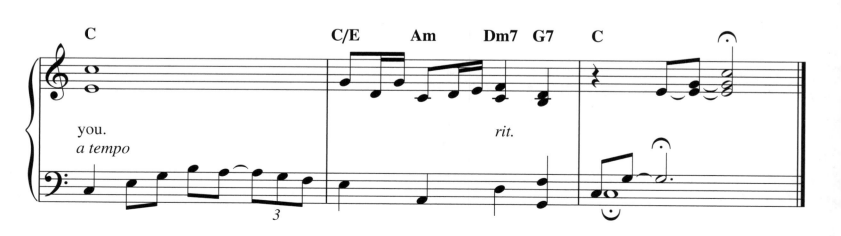

you.   *rit.*
a tempo

WHAT CHILD IS THIS?

Traditional
Arranged by DAVID FOSTER
and ERIN TAYLOR FOSTER

Whom an - gels greet_____ with an - thems__

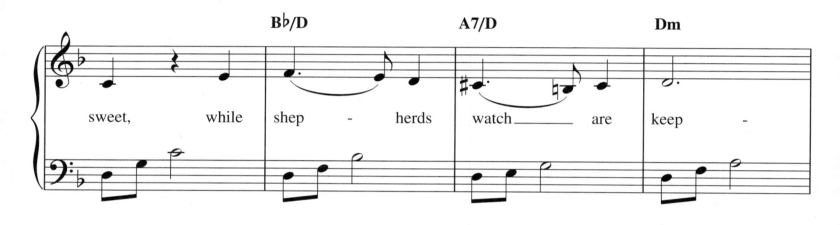

sweet, while shep - herds watch_____ are keep -

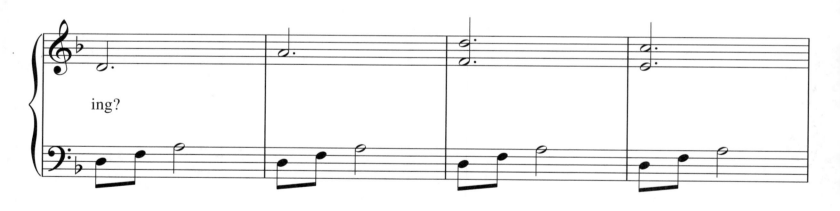

ing?

So bring Him

in - cense, gold and myrhh; come peas - ant,

king,_____ to_____ own_____ Him._____ The King of

kings_____ sal - va - tion brings; let lov - ing

hearts_____ en - throne Him. This,

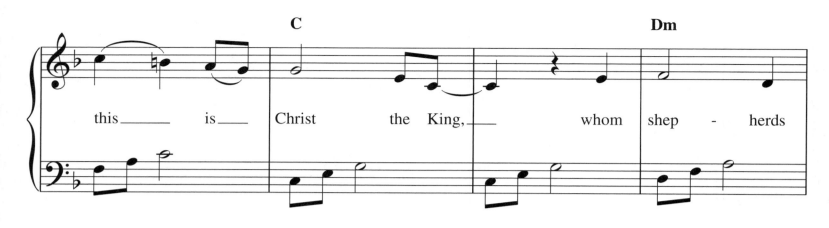

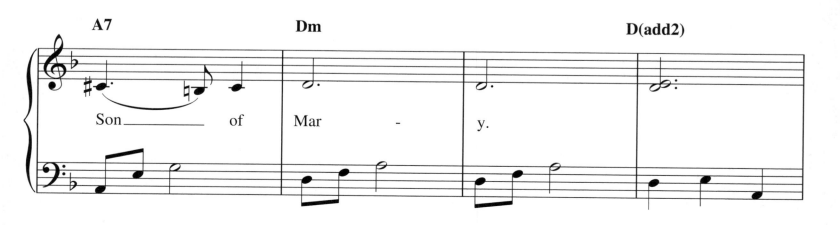

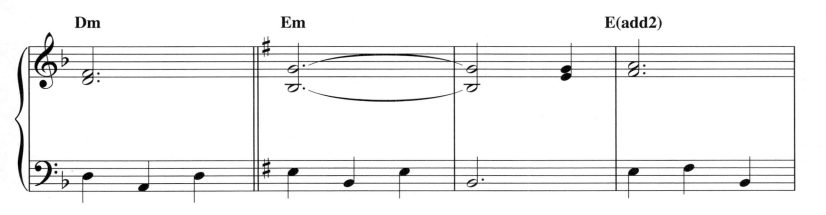

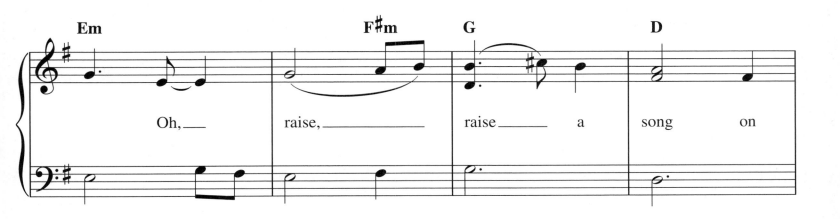

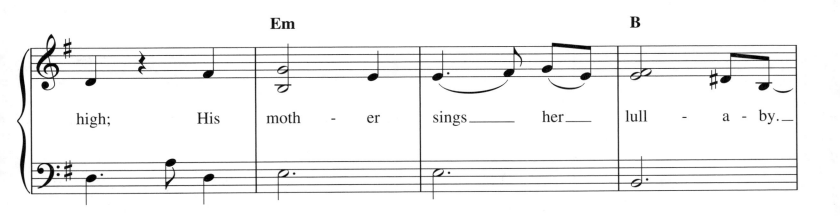

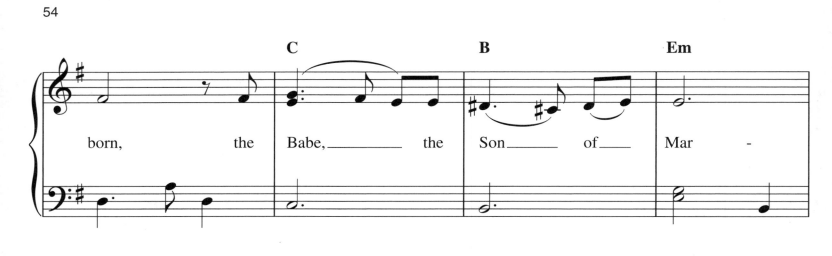

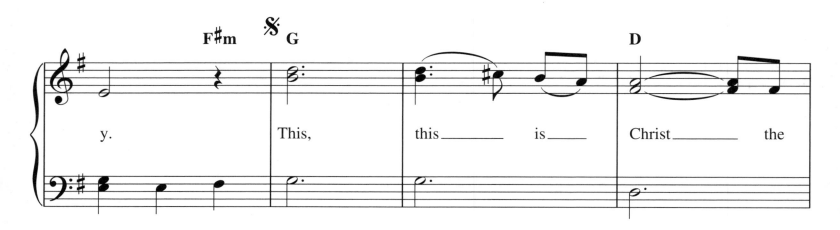

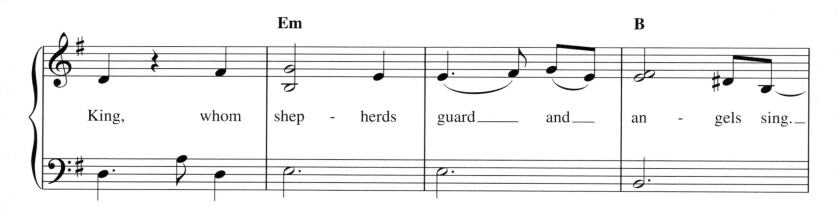

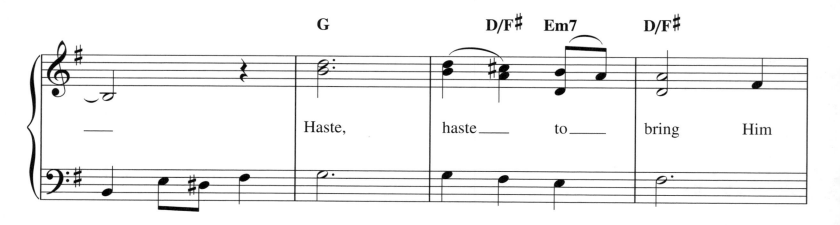

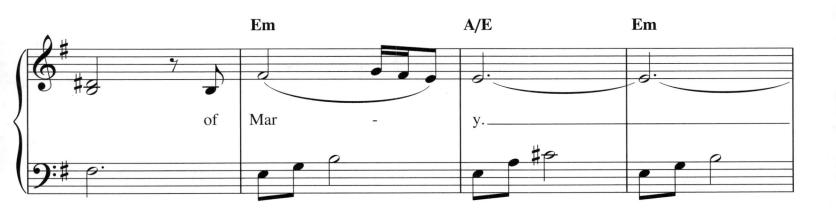

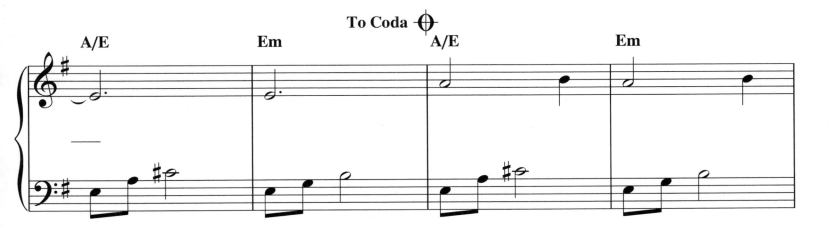

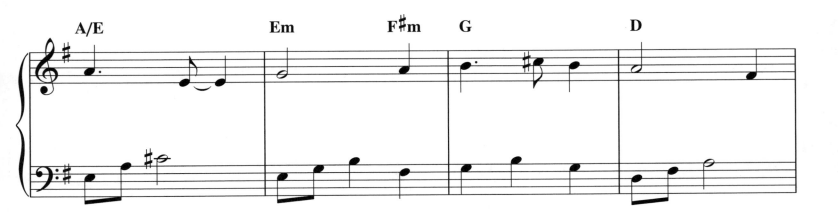

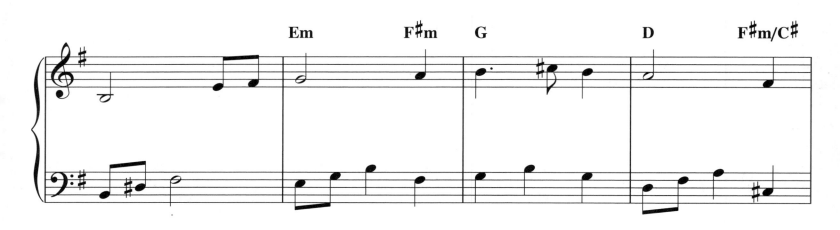

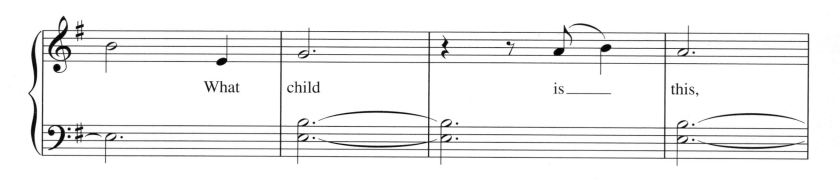

What child is____ this,

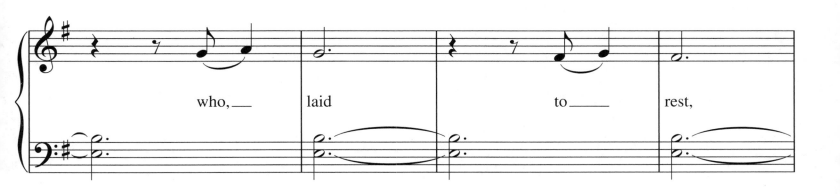

who,___ laid   to___ rest,

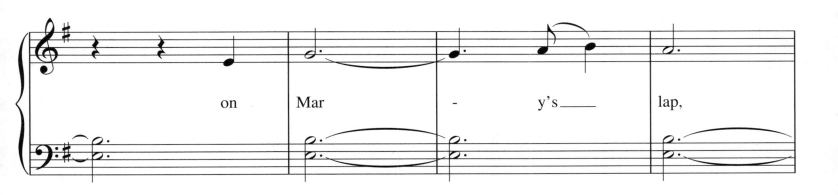

on Mar -   y's___   lap,

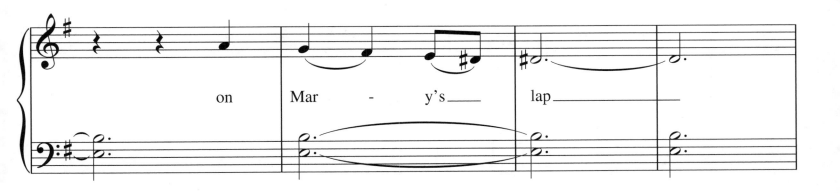

on Mar - y's___   lap___

D.S. al Coda

CODA

A/E

He is sleep - ing.___

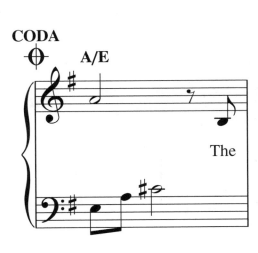

The

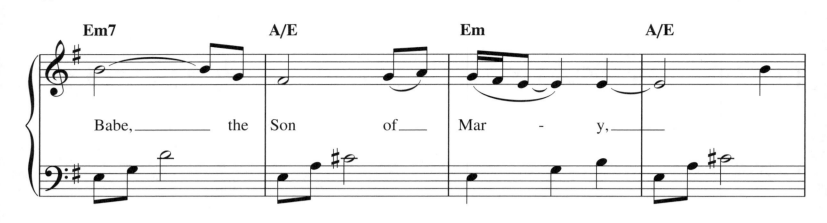

Babe,_____ the Son of____ Mar - y,_____

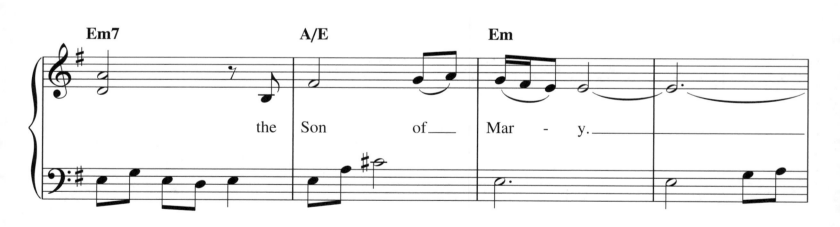

the Son of____ Mar - y._____

THE FIRST NOËL

Traditional
Arranged by DAVID FOSTER,
JOCHEM VAN DER SAAG and KIRK FRANKLIN

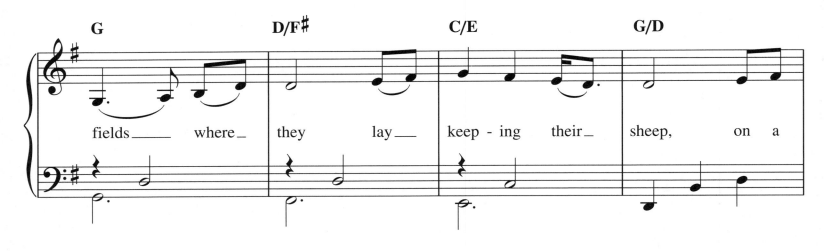

fields_____ where__ they lay__ keep - ing their__ sheep, on a

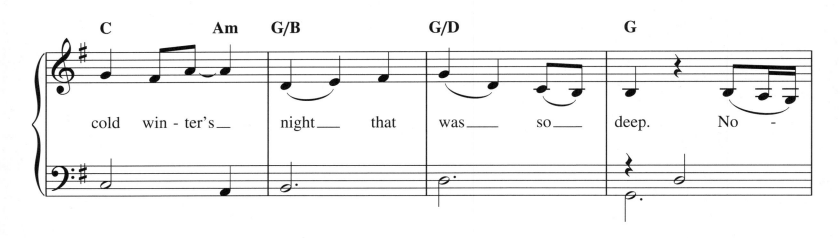

cold win - ter's__ night___ that was___ so___ deep. No -

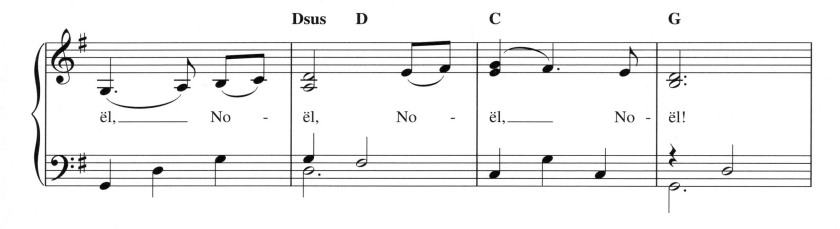

ël,_____ No - ël, No - ël,_____ No - ël!

Gospel groove
Gmaj9

Born is the___ King___ of___ Is - ra - el!_____

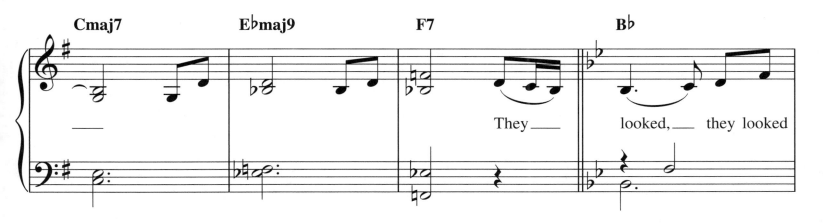

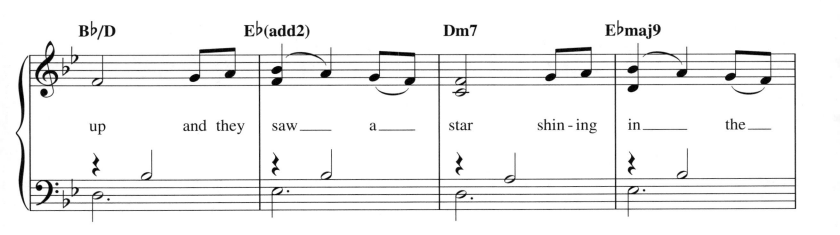

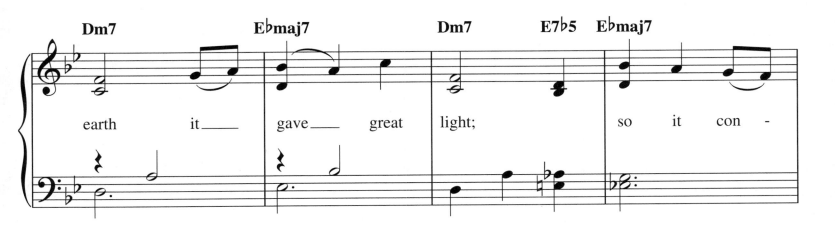

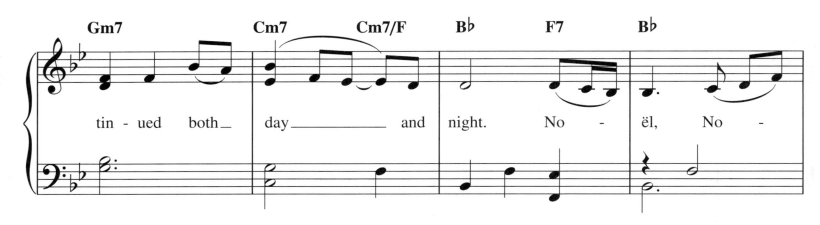

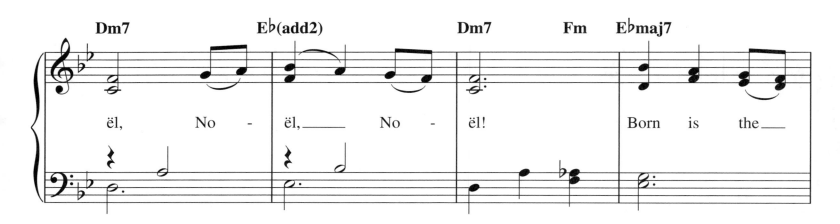

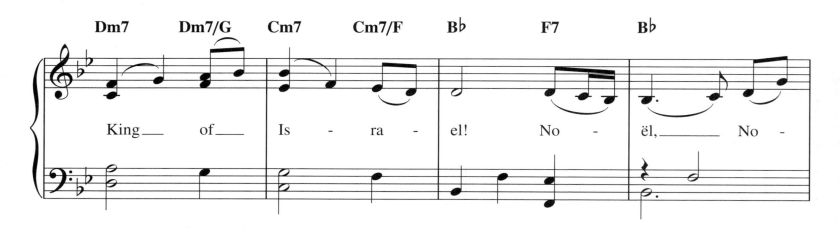

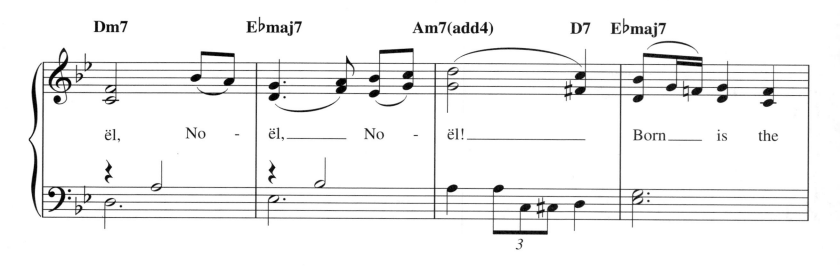

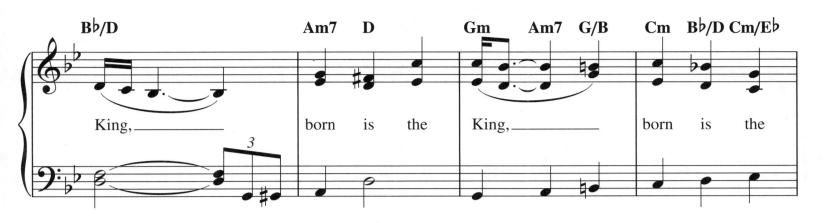

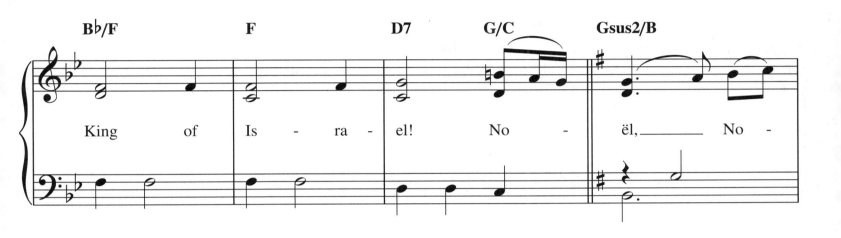

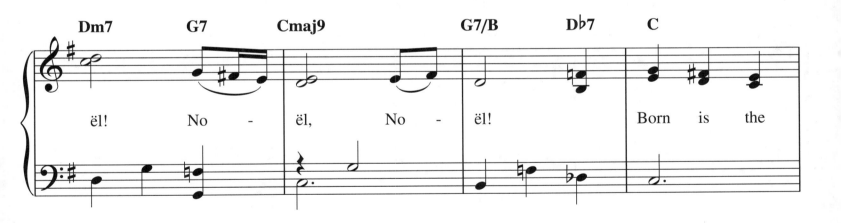

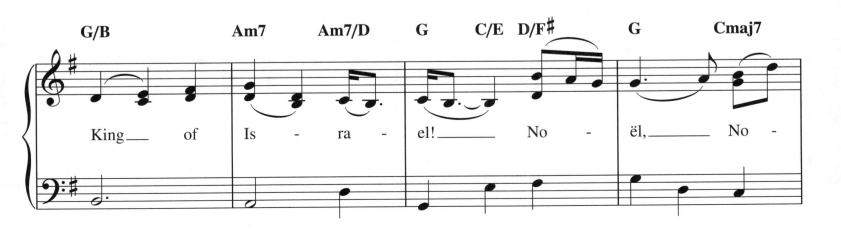

64

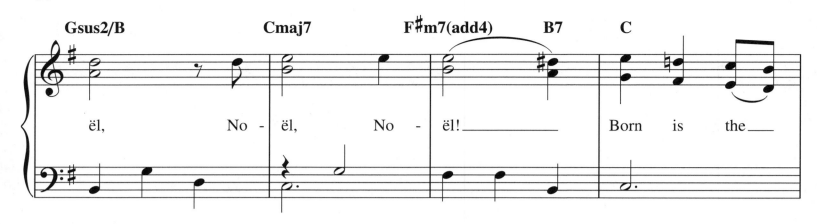

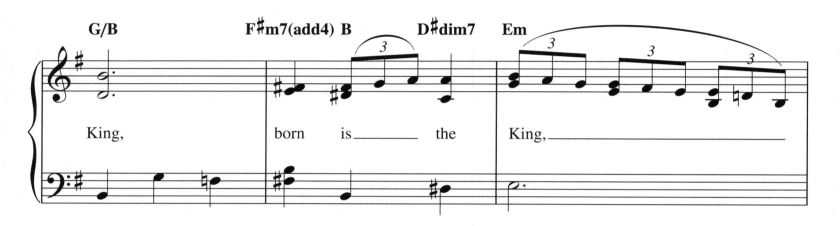

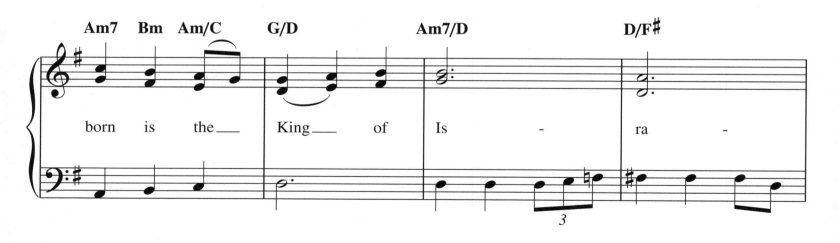

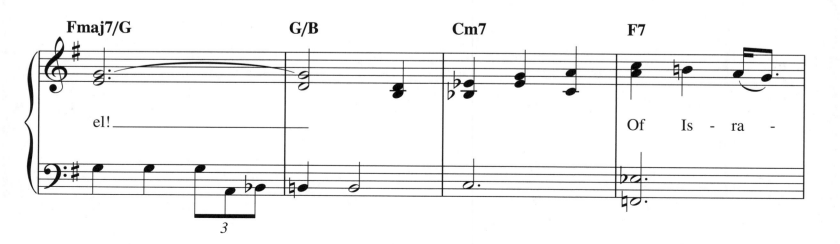

PETIT PAPA NOËL

Words and Music by HENRI MARTINET
and RAYMOND OVANESSIAN

C'est la bel- le nuit de No-ël___ la neige é-tend son man-teau blanc___ et les yeux

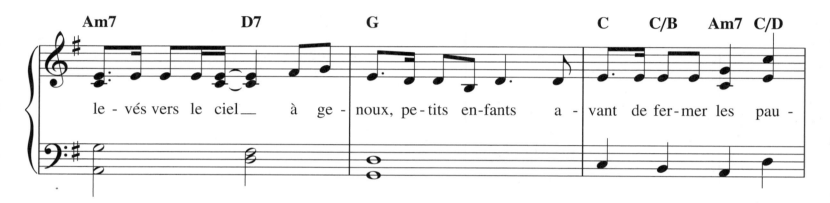

le - vés vers le ciel___ à ge-noux, pe-tits en-fants a - vant de fer-mer les pau -

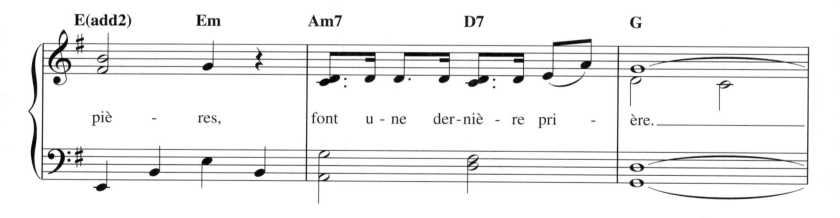

piè - res, font u - ne der-niè-re pri - ère.___

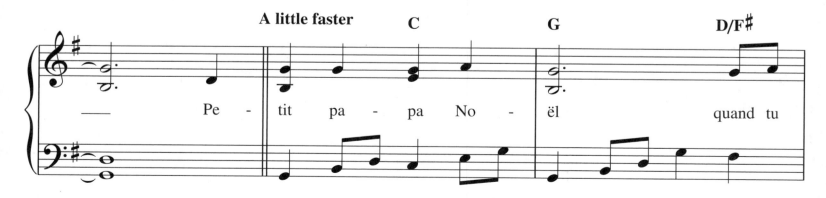

Pe - tit pa - pa No - ël quand tu

de - scen - dras du ciel a - vec des jou - ets par mil-

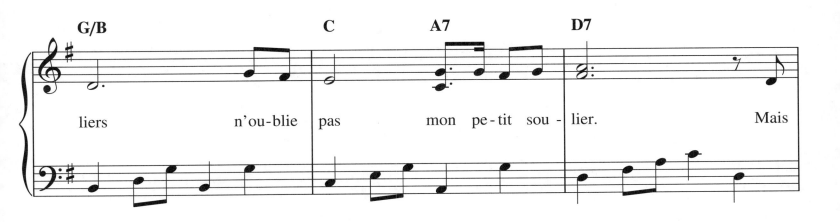

liers n'ou-blie pas mon pe-tit sou - lier. Mais

a - vant de par - tir il fau-dra bien te couv-

rir de - hors tu vas a-voir si froid c'est un

peu   à cause de moi.   Il me tar-de tant   que le
                                      Et quand tu se-ras   sur ton

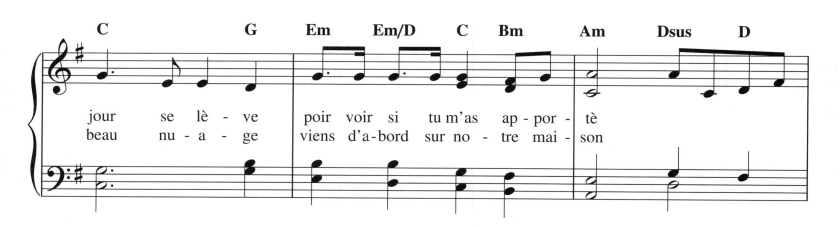

jour se lè - ve   poir voir si tu m'as ap-por-tè
beau nu - a - ge   viens d'a-bord sur no - tre mai-son

To Coda

Tous les beaux jou-joux   que je vois en rê-ve   et que je t'a-i com-man-
Je n'ai pas é - té   tous les jours très sa-ge   mais j'en de-man-de par-

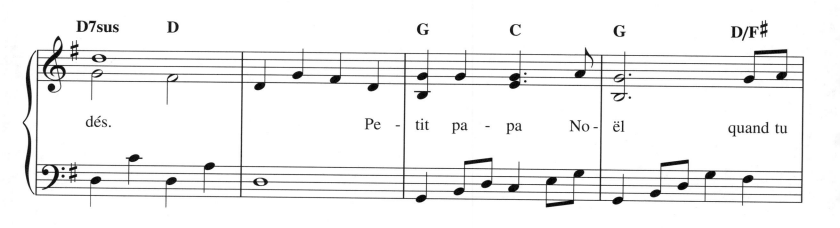

dés.   Pe - tit pa - pa No- ël   quand tu

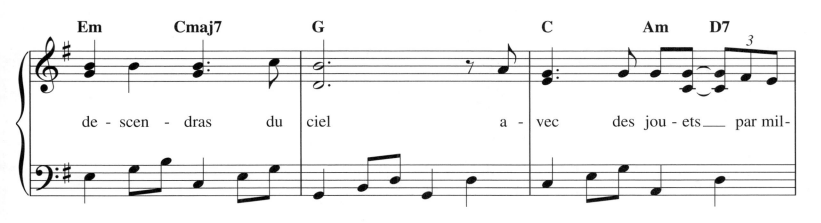

de - scen - dras du ciel a - vec des jou - ets___ par mil-

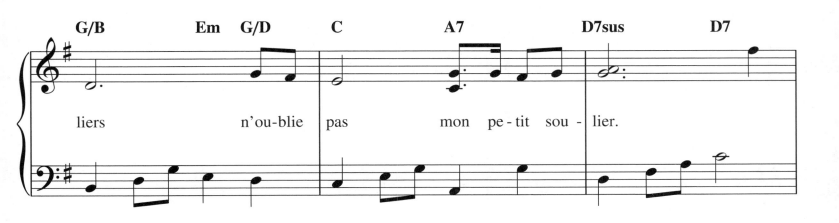

liers n'ou-blie pas mon pe - tit sou - lier.

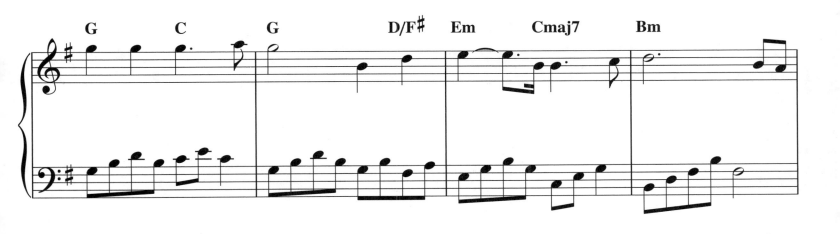

D.S. al Coda

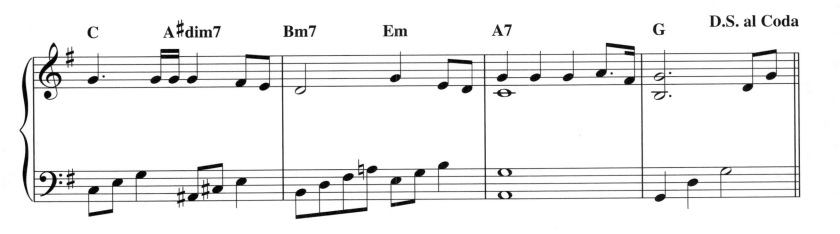

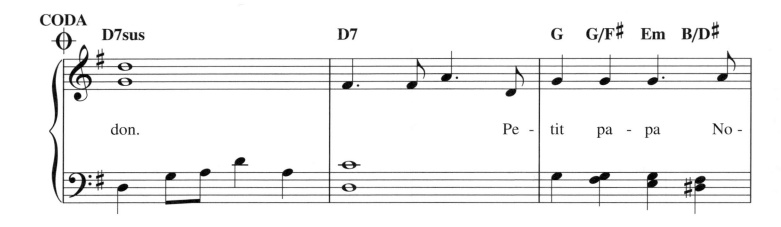

CODA

D7sus — **D7** — **G G/F♯ Em B/D♯**

don. Pe - tit pa - pa No -

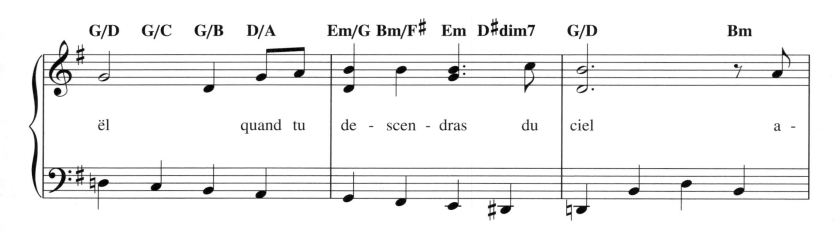

G/D G/C G/B D/A Em/G Bm/F♯ Em D♯dim7 G/D Bm

ël quand tu de - scen - dras du ciel a -

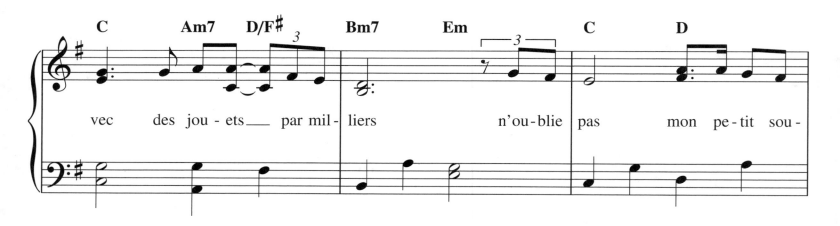

C Am7 D/F♯ Bm7 Em C D

vec des jou - ets__ par mil - liers n'ou - blie pas mon pe - tit sou -

G C Dsus D7 G

lier. Pe - tit pa - pa No - ël.

rit.

IT CAME UPON A MIDNIGHT CLEAR

Traditional
Arranged by DAVID FOSTER
and SARAH MICHAEL FOSTER

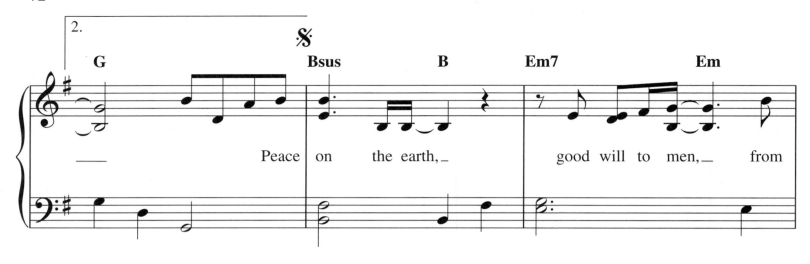

Peace on the earth,_ good will to men,_ from

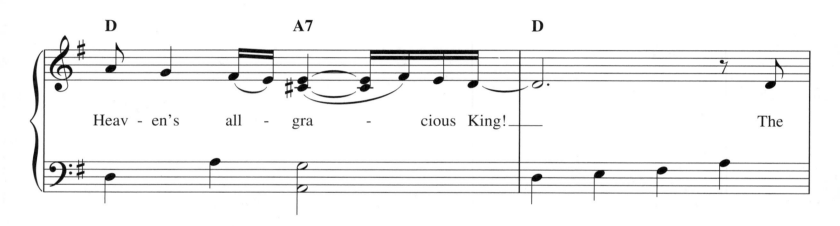

Heav-en's all - gra - cious King!_ The

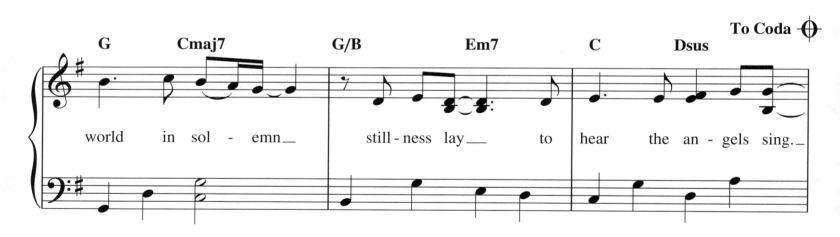

world in sol - emn_ still-ness lay__ to hear the an-gels sing._

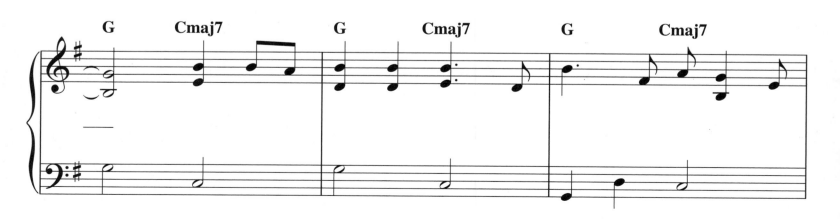

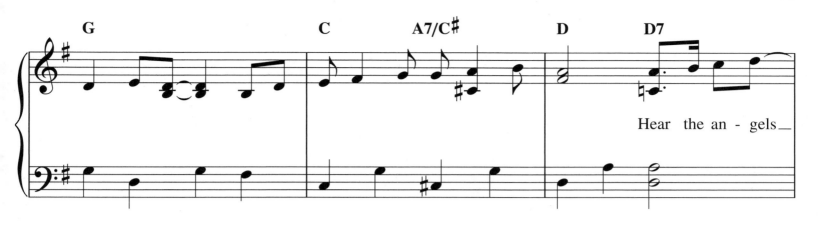

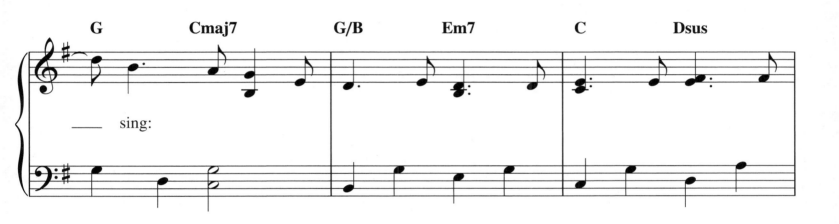

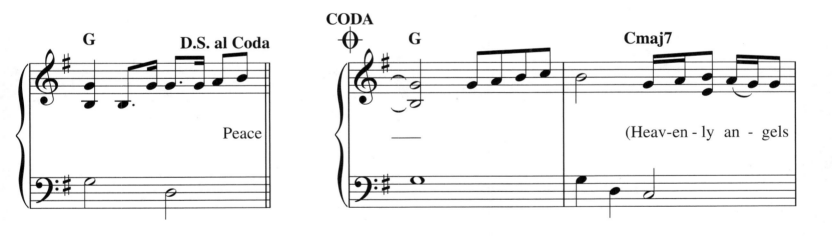

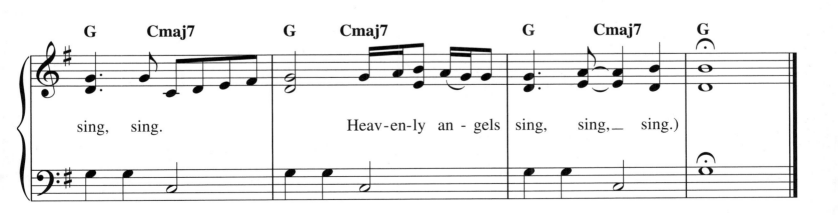

PANIS ANGELICUS

Traditional
Arranged by BILL ROSS
and JOSH GROBAN

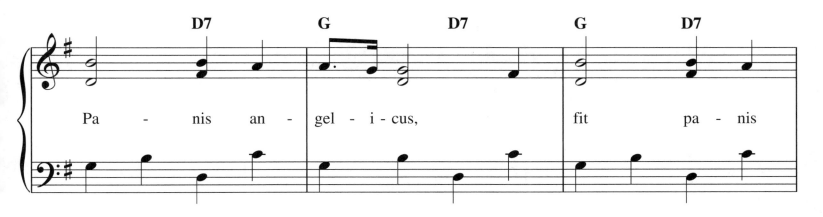

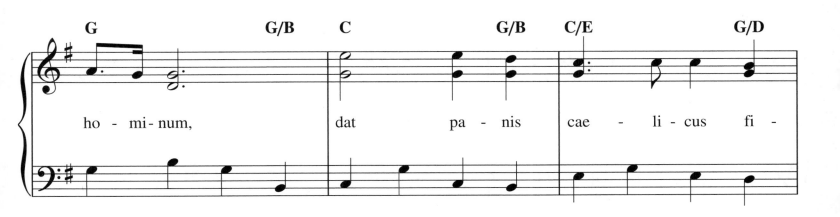

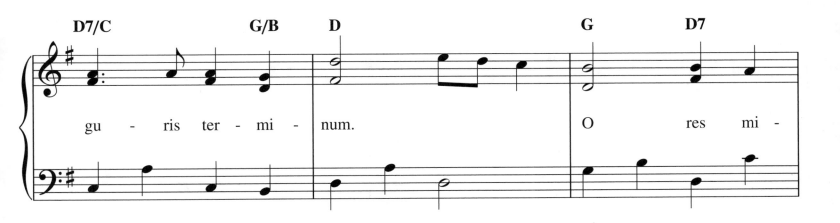

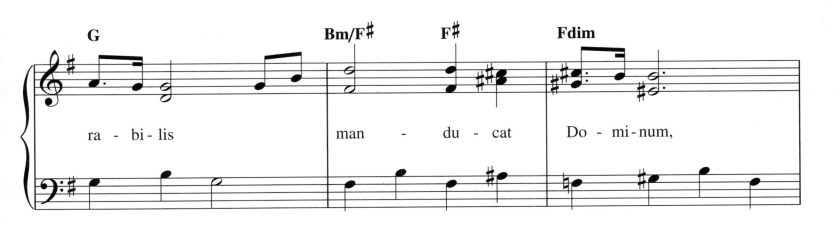

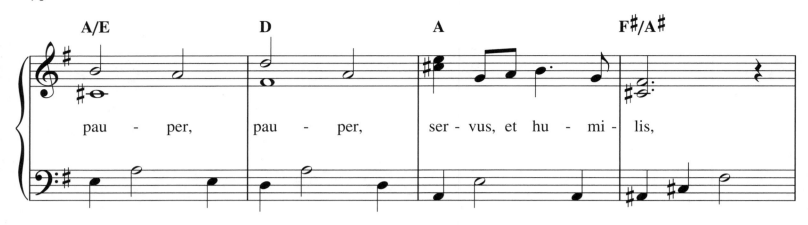

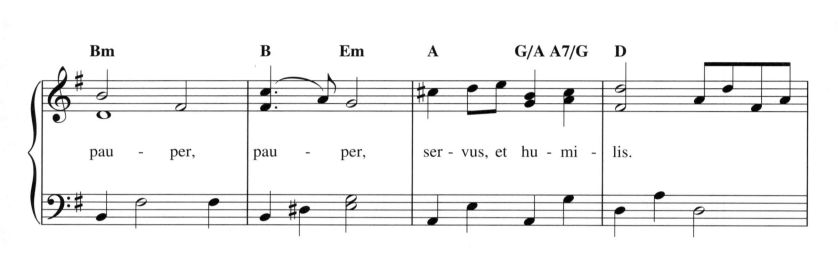

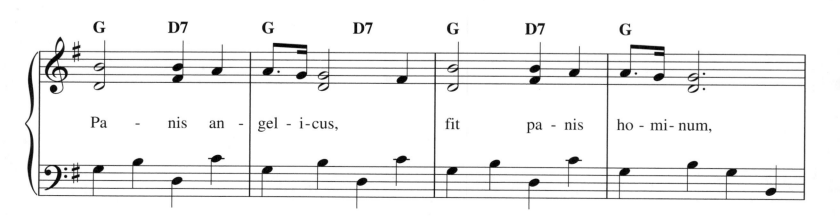

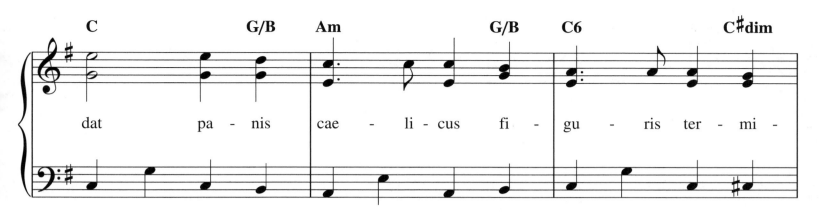

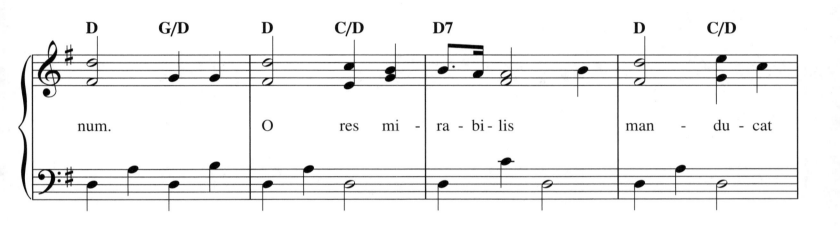

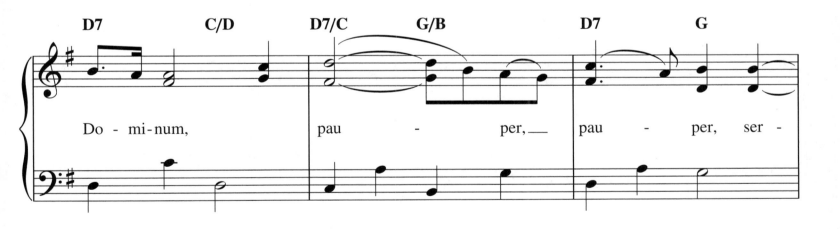

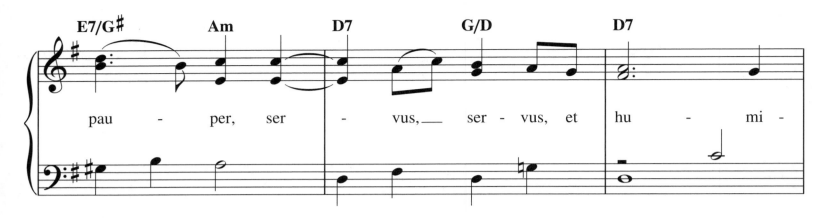

pau - per, ser - vus,__ ser - vus, et hu - mi -

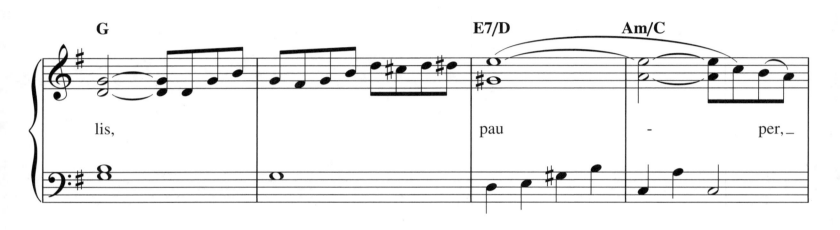

lis, pau - per,__

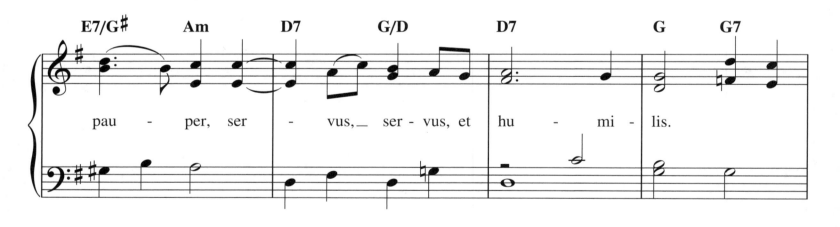

pau - per, ser - vus,__ ser - vus, et hu - mi - lis.

rit.

O COME ALL YE FAITHFUL

Traditional
Arranged by DAVID FOSTER,
JORDAN D. FOSTER and BRADLEY DECHTER

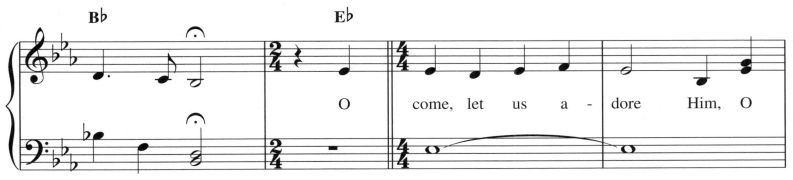

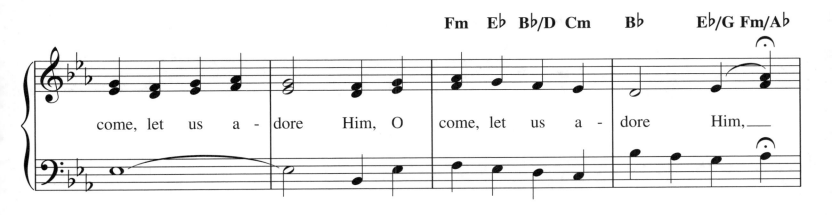

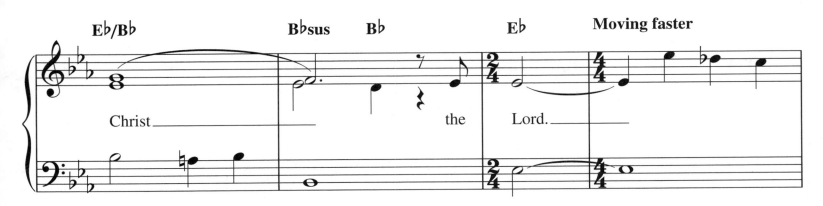

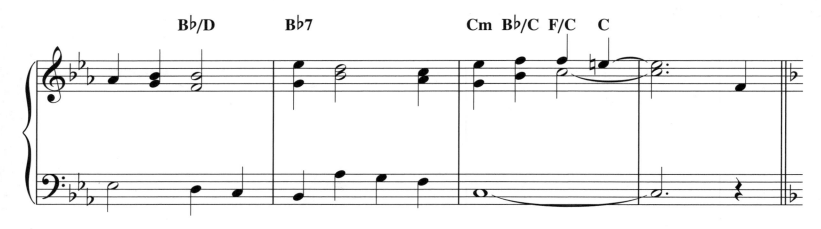

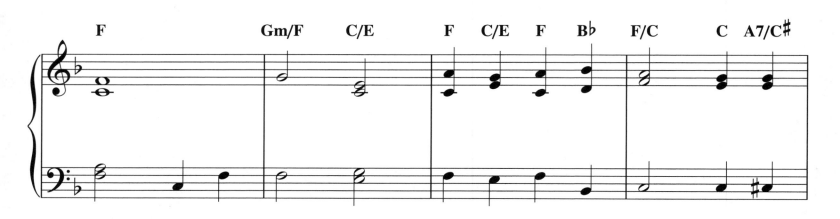

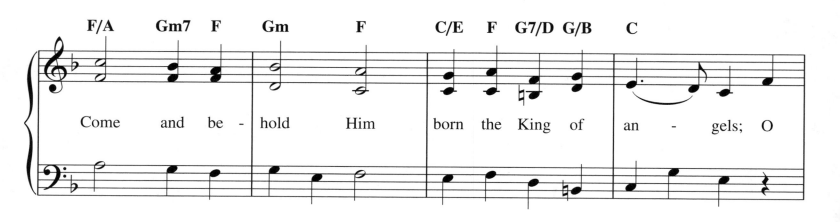

Come and be - hold Him born the King of an - gels; O

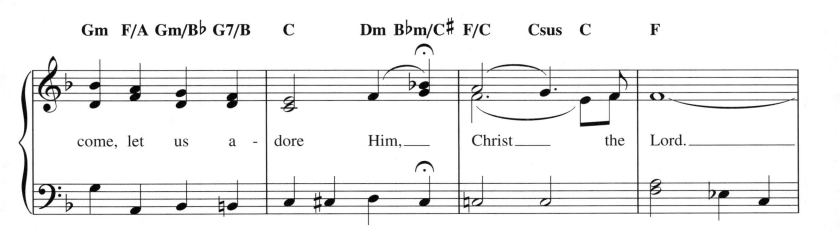

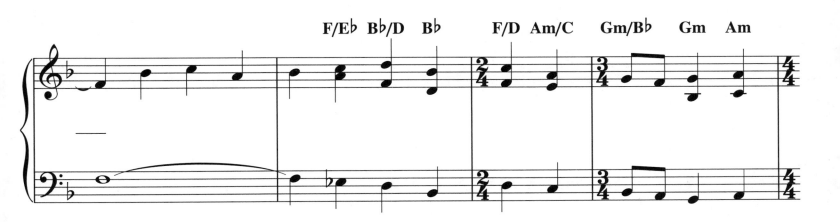

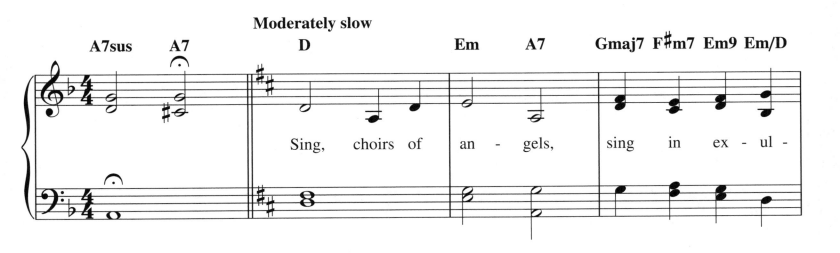

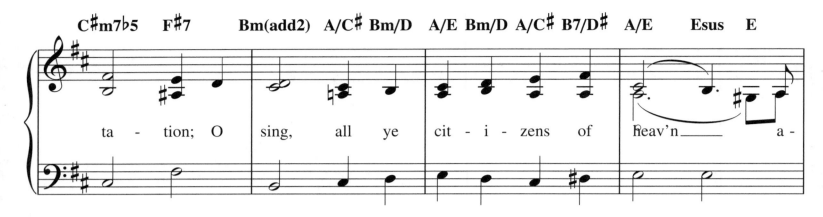

82

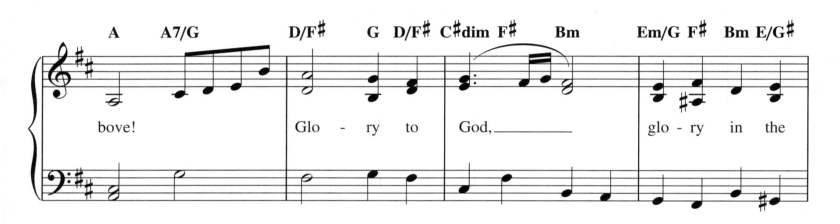

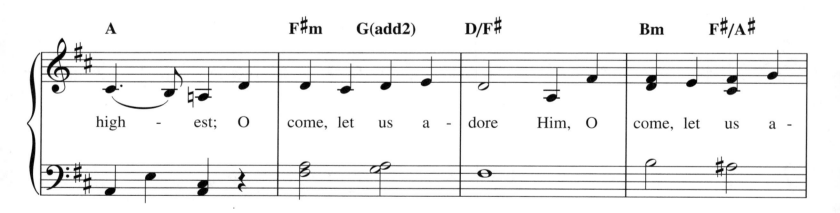

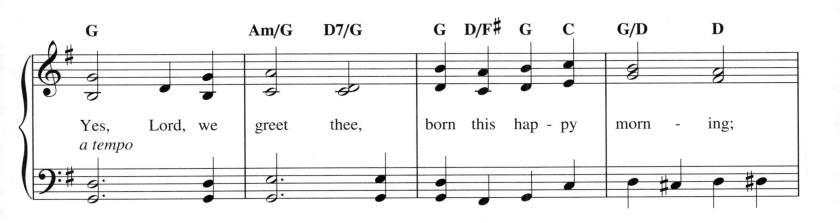

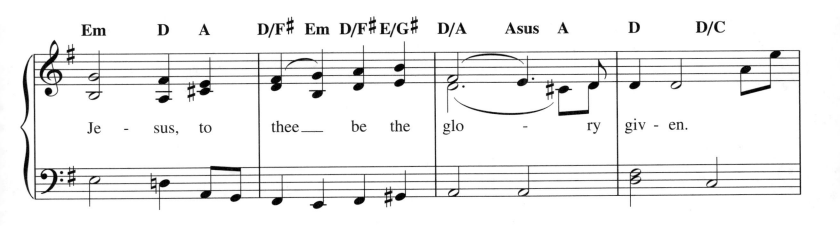

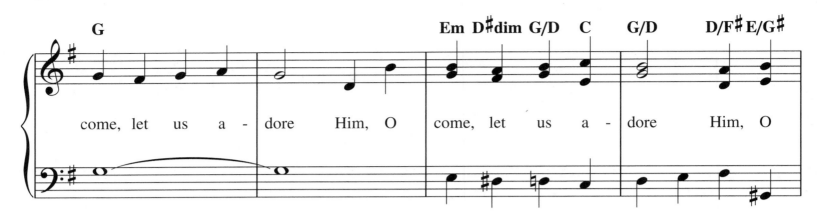

come, let us a - dore Him, O come, let us a - dore Him, O

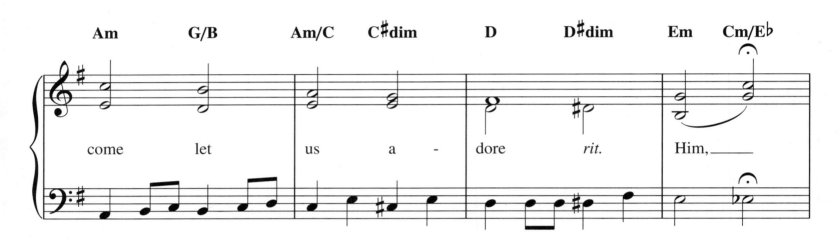

come let us a - dore *rit.* Him,_____

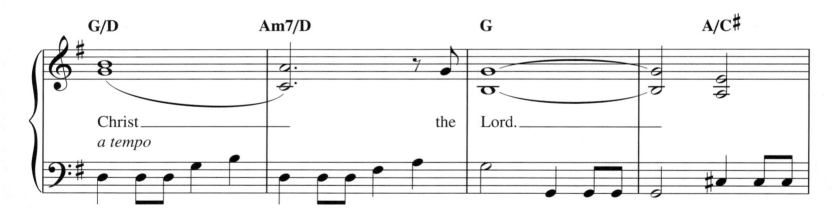

Christ_____ the Lord._____
a tempo

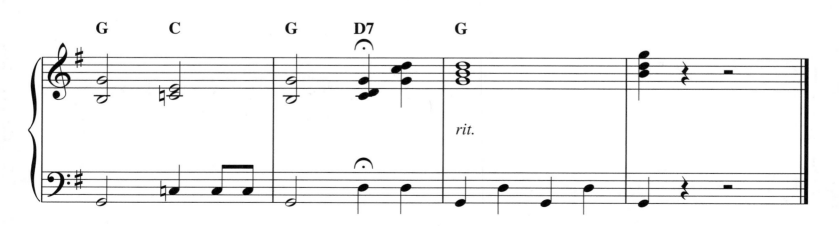

rit.